THE GRAIL CASTLE
AND ITS MYSTERIES

The Grail Castle

AND ITS MYSTERIES

by

LEONARDO OLSCHKI

*translated from the Italian by
J. A. Scott and edited, with a
foreword, by Eugène Vinaver*

UNIVERSITY OF CALIFORNIA PRESS
BERKELEY AND LOS ANGELES 1966

University of California Press
Berkeley and Los Angeles
California

First published in Italy in 1961 in
Atti dell' Accademia Nazionale dei Lincei,
Rome, under the title 'Il castello del Re
Pescatore e i suoi misteri nel *Conte del
Graal* di Chrétien di Troyes', and now
published in English by permission of
the Academy

Printed in Great Britain

Contents

Foreword

LEONARDO OLSCHKI's death in December 1961 de-
prived Romance scholarship of one of its leading figures.
Born in Verona in 1885, he began his academic work with
a Heidelberg dissertation on Guarini's *Pastor Fido* and its
influence in Germany (1908). Five years later appeared
his monograph entitled *Der ideale Mittelpunkt Frankreichs
im Mittelalter*, which still ranks as a classic. It was followed
by *Paris nach den altfranzösischen nationalen Epen* and in
the late twenties by *Die romanischen Literaturen des
Mittelalters*—two characteristic syntheses of the literary
history of Romance countries. 'Romania' to Olschki was
a reality, not just a convenient grouping of languages,
and it was his belief in its existence as a coherent cultural
unit that inspired, among other things, his famous
Struttura spirituale e linguistica del mondo neolatino (1935)
and his *Genius of Italy*, first published in America in 1949
and recently reissued in an Italian version (*L'Italia e il suo
genio*, 1953 and 1964). But his range was even wider than
these titles suggest. Between 1919 and 1927 he wrote his
three-volume *Geschichte der neusprachlichen wissenschaft-
lichen Literatur*, and in 1937 added to it a literary history
of geographical discovery (*Storia letteraria delle scoperte
geografiche*). Through his interest in Marco Polo he
became a student of Far-Eastern culture, and his *Marco
Polo's Precursors* (1943) prepared the ground for a more
ambitious work, *L'Asia di Marco Polo* (1957), as well as
for his *Guillaume Boucher, a French Artist at the court of the*

Khans (1946). Last but not least, he was one of the first philologists to be aware of the links between literature and the visual arts in the Middle Ages, witness his work on the French illuminated manuscripts; and it was through an example of medieval sculpture, the famous Modena archivolt, that he first became interested in the problem of the origins of Arthurian romance.

The essay which is here offered in an abridged English translation by Mr J. A. Scott, himself an Italian scholar, was published in the Acts of the Lincei Academy in 1961 (*Atti*, X: 3, 101–59) under the title: *Il castello del Re Pescatore e i suoi misteri nel 'Conte del Graal' di Chrétien di Troyes*. It was Olschki's last published work and a remarkably timely one: not just another addition to the vast literature of the Grail, but a thorough exposition of a theory which had never before been put forward with such an abundance of supporting evidence. Chrétien de Troyes' *Conte del Graal* is interpreted here 'as a drama between heresy and faith, damnation and redemption, with the final victory assured for the latter'; it is linked 'with some of the most dramatic occurrences in contemporary French civilization'. And yet no one will deny that for the student of medieval literature the great attraction of this essay lies in the fact that throughout the elaborate investigation of the Grail theme and its possible sources the poet is always remembered and the integrity of the poem scrupulously respected. The critic is well aware that whatever may be said about the relationship between the work and its intellectual and cultural background, its main constituent elements belong to another sphere: 'The grail procession, its various symbols and

characters, the subtle psychological insights which reveal
profound human experience, both of maternal and profane love . . . all this and much besides is pure poetry and
not folklore or erudition: original creation and not
pedantic imitation. Any attempt to penetrate further into
the secrets of a poet of passion and feeling is vain curiosity
rather than enlightened criticism. We must be satisfied
with an understanding of the inspiration and purpose of
this work.' Whatever the practical value of Olschki's
interpretation it is certainly the one which combines most
successfully the two essential, yet seemingly contradictory
approaches to literary exegesis: the placing of the work in
its context and the discovery of its autonomous nature.
To Olschki these two approaches, far from being in-
compatible, are complementary, and this is the reason
why his theory about the meaning of the Grail mysteries
seems, at least to one reader, to be more convincingly
argued than any that has so far been advanced. He was
sufficiently well versed in medieval literary and intellectual history to know the kind of criticism to which
such a theory was open. He knew that in writing about
the hidden meaning of a medieval romance one ran the
risk of discovering that it had no hidden meaning; that
the puzzle he was trying to solve, if there was a puzzle,
had been left unsolved by the poet, since *Perceval* was an
unfinished work; and he knew above all that his interpretation of the work as an attempt to rescue the characters
from heretic rites and beliefs could be countered by the
view that the goal of Perceval's endeavour was on the
contrary to surmount the pride of chivalry and the joy of
earthly love. Perhaps—and this again Olschki knew as

well as anyone else—if both views are questioned, there is
room for a more comprehensive one, which provides a
place for those attached to active life as well as for those
who flee the world. In a twelfth-century narrative poem
written by so skilful a dialectician as Chrétien de Troyes
contradictory interpretations are never mutually exclusive,
and if a hypothesis such as Olschki's has a serious claim to
our attention, it is not because it is exhaustive, but because
it illumines at least one vital aspect of Chrétien's most
puzzling work.

A study of such importance by one of the few men of
our time capable of speaking of medieval civilization in
the full sense of the term was too great an event to be con-
signed to the relative obscurity of the Acts of an Academy:
it had to be made known to the ever-widening circle of
readers not content to hear about such things at second-
hand. For their convenience we have included, as the
author himself had done, the two relevant extracts from
Alfons Hilka's edition of Chrétien's text; we have re-
produced the critical notes accompanying the essay; and
we have added to the Bibliography a list of the main
studies and reviews of *The Grail Castle* that have appeared
since its publication. Armed with this material the reader
will be able to approach the problem with as much
attention to detail as Olschki invariably displayed in his
own work, and with a mind as open as his always was.
There is no better way of serving his memory than to read
him as he read his texts: with gratitude for our enlighten-
ment and with critical understanding.

EUGÈNE VINAVER

The Grail Castle and its Mysteries[1]

THE theme of the Grail and of its accompanying mysteries is without doubt the most disturbing and difficult of all the problems that medieval literature presented to contemporary readers and handed down to the curiosity of later ages. And such it has remained in its numerous developments in both prose and verse throughout the centuries, since Chrétien de Troyes first inserted it, about the year 1180, in his famous romance in rhymed verse that treats of *Perceval ou le Conte del Graal*. The importance of this episode in the well-nigh inextricable texture of the poem is thus revealed in its title.

The episode, which consists of only 222 lines, is one of the briefest among the 9,284 that make up the romance to which it has given its name and which was, it would seem, interrupted by the author's death. Its sequel is just as brief (ll. 6387–518), while we find nothing of importance in between that has any direct bearing on it.[a] Chrétien, it would seem, did not even invent this fable, since he states that he has set down in rhyme a 'livre' that had been given to him for this purpose by 'the good Count Philip' (l. 53) of Flanders, originally from Alsace, who died on the battlefield near St John of Acre in June 1191.[b] It is difficult to doubt the truth of this assertion, since the poet would certainly not have dared to make a public pronouncement that could have been denied to his discomfiture by such a

[1] Superior letters (*a*, *b*, *c*) refer to the Notes at the end of the volume. Superior figures (¹, ²) refer to footnotes.

powerful and famous lord, who outlived him by several years. Nothing, however, is known about this book; and every conjecture regarding its contents, language and form must remain mere speculation.

We shall not attempt to explore the doubtful origins of what Chrétien himself describes as *la matière* of his romances in general and of this one in particular. We shall limit our investigation to what he calls its *sen* or meaning: namely, to that part of the Grail story which certainly owes its creation and interpretation to him.[a] As a result of this distinction, the poem appears as an obscure allegory to which we have lost the key. It is to this meaning that these pages are dedicated in the hope that they may serve as a point of departure for further investigation of the mystery with which the French author deliberately surrounded his poem.

It may be well to recall the manner in which the episode of the Grail is introduced by him in his romance. Perceval, the orphaned son of a lord who died from wounds received in battle, has inherited his father's knightly qualities (l. 1480). He has lost two brothers—the victims of chivalric adventures—and leaves his mother while still a youth. The latter, in order to preserve him from the fate that had befallen his brothers, had brought him up in complete ignorance of his social condition and of all religious practices. Since, however, she is unable to restrain his passion for adventure, she gives him, after his meeting with five knights from Arthur's court, some wise and pious counsel which is an expression of chivalric morality: namely, to serve ladies and offer up prayers to God. She also makes a brief allusion to the Passion of Jesus Christ and admonishes him to visit churches and monasteries. However, he does not know what these are or what purpose they serve, and receives no specific information regarding the Eucharist and eternal salvation.[a]

In fact, this youth comes to know Jesus Christ merely as a *prophete sainte* (l. 581) or as *cel seignor* (l. 593), while, like the pagans and heretics, he remains ignorant of His divine essence.[b] As the whole romance will show, this ingenuous young man has only a vague religious sense, which is never embodied in canonical forms or given outward expression in the practices of Christian worship. Placing more faith in his javelins than in divine aid, he even refuses to make the sign of the cross (ll. 118–20). The extent to which his Catholic faith is and remains uncertain is revealed, among other things, by the fact that after years of varied experience he does not even know when or what Good Friday is and thus excites the indignation and protests of some penitent knights whom he meets on this day in the forest where his conversion will shortly take place (ll. 6264 f.). He may invoke and sometimes pray to God or swear *par le Sauveor . . . an cui je croi* (ll. 172–3); but the conventional phrases he uses do not involve him in any way.[c] His positive knowledge of the supernatural is limited to what he has heard of God as supreme beauty (ll. 144–5), of the splendour of the angels and of the horror of the devils. When he first meets with a group of knights and hears the great noise made by their arms, he mistakes them for devils—*les plus laides choses del mont* (l. 116)—and then, upon seeing them resplendent in the sunlight, for angels whom he knows to be

> Les plus beles choses qui soient
> Fors Deu qui est plus biaus que tuit.
>
> (ll. 144–5)

Naïvely enchanted by this apparition, he goes on to ask one of them whether he is perchance God Himself, *einsi luisanz et einsi fais*, or even more beautiful than He.

This may seem to be a somewhat childish conception of the Godhead. But with its aesthetic accents unknown to preceding ages, it is characteristic of Chrétien's times, when the image of the deity had begun to assume in sculpture the ideal type of the 'beau Dieu'.[a] Moreover, his contemporaries could not have failed to notice in the contrast between the angels and devils certain overtones to which their ears were far better attuned than ours. For not only did the concept of God as luminous beauty and the angels as His resplendent creation, or—less correctly —emanation, impress the theologians of that age more forcibly than it had done at any previous time, but the heretical sects of the Gnostic–Manichaean tradition made it the pivot of their theological speculations by concentrating their doctrines of morality and salvation in the God of Light.[b]

As a result, both Catholic orthodoxy and Catharist heresy had intensified traditional demonology in the metaphysical contrast between light and darkness as cosmic concepts.[c] These were set forth in various treatises and influenced the fine arts and poetry down to Dante's day and beyond: an obvious expression of the religious unrest and intense search for God that are characteristic of this age of spiritual, artistic, and moral renovation. We find proof of this in Wolfram von Eschenbach's *Parzifal*, composed in the first years of the thirteenth century, in which the German poet closely follows the poem of Chrétien de Troyes in narrating the 'enfances' of his hero, although he obviously does not lack originality.[a] Far more explicit than the French poet, Wolfram makes his *Parzifal* ask the question that tormented the hearts and minds of countless people in those centuries, oppressed as they were by religious doubt in their search for a new faith: namely, *ōwē, muoter, waz ist got?* (Alas, mother, what is God?).[b] And the reply he obtains to this desperate question is not that which an orthodox Catholic would have given him: it bears the mark of the dualism characteristic of the heresies that had spread in the twelfth century through France, Italy, and even Germany, as the ultimate Western ramifications of the tenacious Manichaean doctrines. God is light, brighter than the light of day, in utter contrast to the demons of the infernal darkness:

> sun, ich sage dirz āne spot
> er ist noch liehter denne der tac . . .
> sīn muoter underschiet im gar
> daz vinster unt daz lieht gevar.[c]

This is the concept which, in Chrétien's poem, is responsible for the mistake made by the ingenuous youth upon perceiving Arthur's resplendent knights. Destined to search for God, he immediately makes his way to the king's court in his rustic Welsh dress, while his mother, seeing him go towards his destiny, falls to the ground *al chief del pont* and dies of a broken heart. In this lively exordium the poet discreetly shows us, on the one hand, the spiritual basis of the whole romance which Wolfram understood and illustrated so well; on the other, his hero's inner drama, since he had involuntarily become guilty of a sin that will weigh upon his soul for the rest of his life and that he will have to expiate through confession and absolution.[1]

The poem's two basic themes are thus set forth at the very beginning: the *metaphysical* concept of the immanent antithesis between the god of light, who *ex nihilo creavit suos angelos*, and the god of darkness, who created the world and man;[a] and the *moral* motif that asserts the fatality of sin as the work of destiny and not of man's free will, the fatality to which Perceval unwittingly falls victim, while he remains unchanged by any experience of life and education.[b] Seen in this light he would appear quite different from the numskull he has usually been made out to be by modern interpreters of the poems of Chrétien de Troyes and Wolfram von Eschenbach: the 'Dümmling' of the German critics, the 'simpleton' of Anglo-American scholars, and the 'sot' of the French: 'le sot dont la bêtise l'empêche de faillir.'[2] We would simply ask: did the poet really need such a complicated series of events, mysteries, and symbols in order to relate the story of a perfect fool with the moral intentions expressed in the prologue? To suppose this is to be guilty of injustice against both the author and his hero, who is not incorrigibly foolish but, quite simply, an innocent

---

[1] This occurs after five long years of adventure, through the good offices of a hermit uncle of his (ll. 6342–513) in the way described below.

[2] René Nelli, *Lumière du Graal*, Paris, 1951, p. 29.

soul at grips with the realities of life, his own destiny, and the mystery that surrounds man.

It is difficult to believe that such an ingenuous youth, who bungles everything and brings bad luck wherever he goes, could be the haphazard protagonist of a French romance that opens with the promise of a rich moral reward for the reader; and then of a German poem which, from the very first verse, recalls the dangers of doubt (*zwīvel*) and teaches the way to leave Satan's gloomy kingdom and arrive at the light of wisdom.[a] Phrases such as these are not mere metaphors; they form part of a language fashioned by doctrines and sentiments characteristic of the age to which the two outstanding poets of the Perceval saga belong; and the sporadic echoes of these doctrines and sentiments in contemporary Troubadour lyric convey spiritual uncertainty and a desire for a renewal rather than adherence to the heretical doctrines of the time.[b]

After the dramatic and significant exordium that serves as a point of departure for the narration of Perceval's adventures Chrétien gives us the story of his first involuntary errors: the kiss and the ring that he snatches by force from the Maiden of the Tent (which he mistakes for a church), thus provoking her lover to anger and vengeance, since he suspects her of infidelity and punishes her in cruel fashion. It is here that this pure fool, without guile or experience, appears as the victim not only of his mother's well-intentioned advice, which he had not understood, but also of a blind fatality that drives him towards adventure and sin.

Once he has arrived at Arthur's court in his rustic

B

Welsh garb, the hapless youth, driven on by this same impetuosity, kills 'le Chevalier Vermeil' and puts on his red armour, whereby he now becomes a knight *de facto* though not *de jure*. Quick to avenge another maiden who had been brutally outraged and wounded by Keu, the court steward, he proceeds to the castle of Gornemant de Gorhaut. This episode concludes his martial training with a long speech and reveals how much wisdom and dexterity he had hitherto lacked to be a perfect knight; it also represents his moral investiture after his informal courtly recognition by King Arthur. It culminates in the counsel not to speak too much, to help men, women, and orphans in need, to go to church, to lead a Christian life, and not to make constant reference to his mother.[1]

Yet his first thought is to set out in search of her, since he does not know whether she is dead or alive. Moreover, he does not set foot in a church, either on his own account or on another's advice—and after five years as a wanderer he confesses to a hermit, his uncle, that he has never thought of God or visited any sanctuary.[2] This puts an end to adventures which are exclusively worldly and profane and are recounted in the characteristic romance style of the poet's preceding works, such as *Cligès*, *Lancelot*, and *Yvain*, a style which was to be perpetuated in the *ambages pulcherrimae* of other tales down to Ariosto, the Spanish prose romances, and those of the French Baroque. The pattern is set by the story of Blancheflor, Gornemant's niece, who has long been importuned by Clamadeus des Isles. When Perceval over-

[1] ll. 1639–84.
[2] ll. 6217–23.

comes him in single combat and thus sets free this beautiful princess, she, already enamoured of him, is far more generous with her favours than he with his advances. This is, of course, a conventional theme in the whole of this literary genre. It was earlier represented in the famous reliefs of the cathedrals at Angoulême, Bari, and Modena, where it illustrates, as in Chrétien's romance, one of the principal chivalric virtues: the defence and conquest of a lady.[a]

*   *   *

After dealing with this trite theme, which was destined to inspire Cervantes' immortal satire some four hundred years later, Chrétien achieves a highly artistic and striking contrast by narrating the most extraordinary adventure to be found in this or any other of his romances: the episode of the Fisher King. Driven on by remorse and by longing for his mother, Perceval continues on his way, with his lance in rest, and soon arrives at some impassably deep water. He sees two men sitting in a boat, one of them catching fish. He is told which path he must take, in order to find shelter in this deserted countryside, and discovers a magnificent castle, where, as soon as he is inside, his weapons and horse are taken from him. Then, clothed in a scarlet cloak, he enters a *sale quarrée*.[b] There Perceval sees a handsome man, full of dignity (*un bel prodome*, l. 3086), near a fire blazing in a monumental bronze fireplace supported by four pillars.[c]

This personage is none other than the fisherman just encountered. It is only later in the poem that he is identified as *le riche Roi Pescheor* (l. 3495) and, much farther on (ll. 6431 f.), as Perceval's uncle. The reader may be struck by the fact that this bed-ridden invalid, even though on a litter, is able to fish in a river at a considerable distance from his castle, and return home before our errant knight. However, this marks the entrance to the kingdom of mystery which is not always subject to the clarity and logic that are generally characteristic of Chrétien's lucid style and invention. He now leads us, for once, into a world of symbols that is ruled by a complex and obscure allegory. Indeed, if we would understand it, even in part, we must consider its every aspect and examine its slightest detail.

To return to our story, hardly has Perceval entered the room and exchanged a few polite words with his invalid host, when he receives from him a magnificent sword stamped with its maker's name.[1] In these courtly sur-roundings such a gift could be a simple gesture, without any particular meaning or hidden purpose. The poet has not revealed any such intent. The sword would seem at this point to complete Perceval's knightly armour with special solemnity; it is a further step towards the fulfil-ment of his martial training.[2]

A quite different, and far more complex meaning must, however, be ascribed to the next scene, in which a whole array of symbols passes before the Fisher King, his court, and the astonished eyes of the young knight, who does not

[1] ll. 3130–85. A cousin of his later tells Perceval (ll. 3658–85) the name of the craftsman who alone will be able to repair it, should it be shattered in battle.

[2] It should be remembered that Perceval had received his first sword from Gornemant de Gorhaut (or Goort), when the latter invested him with a knight's armour (ll. 1632–7).

grasp their significance and yet, in spite of his curiosity, does not even ask for an explanation. A squire (*vaslez*) enters from an adjoining room. Passing between the fireplace and the bed, he holds a white lance halfway up the shaft, while from its iron head a drop of crimson blood falls onto his hand. He is followed by two other handsome squires, bearing richly-decorated golden candelabra, while behind them comes a fair noble maiden who carries in her hands *un graal* (l. 3220) set with the most precious gems, followed by a silver *tailleo(i)r*, borne by another maiden (ll. 3231 and 3567).[1] These objects pass by with every course in front of the two guests who are seated at the banquet table and are served meanwhile the most tasty dishes and exquisite wines.[a] Perceval remains silent and decides to ask for an explanation regarding this *graal trestot descovert* from a squire of the court, a knight younger than he, on the following morning. By that time, however, the whole spell has disappeared like a dream, the court has been dispersed and the castle emptied, except for his horse, which is waiting for him in the courtyard, ready for the journey. And so, since by remaining silent he has missed his one opportunity, neither Perceval nor anyone else will ever discover the hidden meaning of this scene and all its details.

This would seem to suggest that the poet does not look upon these details simply as ornaments, but as features

[1] The first of the two 'tailleors' mentioned at this point follows immediately after the Grail with an obvious symbolic function. The other, which is quite independent, is exclusively intended for service at the king's table, to cut a 'hanche de cerf au poivre'—an act that cannot possibly have any religious or symbolic significance. Cf. A. Hilka's cr. ed., p. 683 n.

replete with a significance that the reader must seek out for himself.[1] Those readers—and they are many—who regard them as Christian, Biblical, or Eucharistic symbols would have us believe that the procession represents a visual fulfilment of the virtually non-existent Christian education of this same Perceval who, shortly before, had been unable to distinguish between the tent of a lovesick girl and a church. The bleeding lance would therefore be that with which *Longinus, unus militum* pierced the side of Christ upon the cross, *et continuo exivit sanguis et aqua*,[2] supposedly found at Antioch in the year 1089. The *graal* would then be a further relic of the Passion—the chalice used at the Last Supper—while the *tailleor* is made to correspond to the paten of the Mass. Finally, the maiden who, in the teeth of every rule of canon law, carries the supposedly holy relic, the Grail, would thus be a personification of the Church. In this way, Biblical, liturgical and allegorical elements of an ecclesiastical and sacred character are supposed to be found in this episode of Chrétien's poem.

Everything would fall nicely into place, if only this apparently orthodox piece of liturgy were not the starting point for a mass of quite profane adventures, which are recounted in characteristic 'romantic' style and inspired by chivalric morality, while they remain utterly unrelated to the teachings and symbols of the Church. The whole 'procession' in fact takes place in a completely secular

[1] The decorative elements, which are so abundant in Wolfram's poem and the other Grail romances, are kept to a minimum in Chrétien's sober, functional descriptions.

[2] The Gospel according to St John, 19: 4, 34.

setting.[1] There is no cross, no liturgical gesture, not one single religious figure, to accompany the supposed relics of Christ's Passion. From the ecclesiastical and orthodox point of view, the procession is even sacrilegious, for it is an accessory to a banquet—in other words, almost a caricature. It is therefore astonishing to think that critics can persist in their wish to interpret it as the Christian initiation of an ignorant young knight and as a fanciful expression of the poet's religious feelings.[2] Similarly, these considerations make it impossible for us to identify Chrétien with a namesake of his who was a canon of the Abbey of Saint-Loup at Troyes; for such a person would never have invented or narrated an episode so repugnant to his faith.[a]

It may well be that Chrétien's description of the bleeding white lance was inspired by the famous relic of Christ's Passion. We must, however, exclude the possibility that he *identified* his lance with it or with that which symbolically accompanies the ceremonial of the Byzantine Mass. The explicit Christianization of the objects borne in procession in the Fisher King's castle is to be found for the first time in the fragmentary *Roman de l'Estoire dou Graal* by Robert de Boron, who came shortly after, and was perhaps a rival of, Chrétien.[b] Neither, however, offers the slightest indication of the function of this lance or gives any clue to the understanding of the symbolic value of the scene as a whole.[c] The Grail, which

[1] The term 'procession' must be understood in its non-religious sense.
[2] It should be noted that the description of the banquet (ll. 3260–325) is far longer and more detailed than that of the procession (ll. 3190–242). Perceval, moreover, is far more interested in the various dishes served (ll. 3334–5) than in the supposedly sacred objects that pass before him.

appears immediately after the lance, carried 'entre ses mains' by an elegant young maiden, is likewise not presented in Chrétien as a specifically sacred object.[a] It would be impossible to insist too much on the fact that it is identified by the poet in generic fashion as '*un graal*' (l. 3220), and that it is therefore the reader's curiosity that is aroused, rather than reverence for a divine mystery. It is only Robert de Boron who identifies it with the chalice of the Last Supper, which was afterwards used by Joseph of Arimathea to gather up the blood of Christ upon the cross.[1] Chrétien describes it as *trestot descovert*, or without a cover, at least during the banqueting scene, so that it is difficult to equate it (as has been done quite recently) with a pyx or ciborium for the consecrated host.[b] It should, moreover, be noted that, since the 'grail' constantly gives forth a most brilliant light from the moment of its first appearance, it must indeed have been *trestot descovert*, and never closed as sometimes happens with ecclesiastical objects.[2]

It is a fatal error to wish at all costs to christianize every detail and even the over-all significance of the episode and so fall back on conclusions that are fundamentally opposed to the inner logic of the account. Since there is not the

[1] Ed. cit., esp. ll. 473–572 and then throughout the rest of the poem, for which see E. Hoepffner's article in *Colloques, etc.*, esp. pp. 98 f. The Christian interpretation of the Grail and its characters originates in this pious and pedestrian *Estoire*, and not in Chrétien's poem, which is to be regarded as a point of departure for some of the main themes, but nothing more.

[2] See Joseph Braun, *Das Christliche Altargerät in seinem Sein und in seiner Entwicklung*, Munich, 1932, esp. pp. 280–347. The interpretation of 'trestot descovert' as 'quite visible' (Jean Frappier, *Bulletin de la Soc. Internationale Arthurienne*, VI, 1954, p. 78) is therefore correct.

slightest reference to Christian liturgy in the whole procession,[a] it would be wise to accept the oft-repeated
definition whereby, according to the learned chronicler
Helinand de Froidmont who wrote in the first years of the
thirteenth century, the word *graal* designated, in its Latin
form *gradalis*, a *scutella lata et aliquantulum profunda*, also
mentioned in other texts, which is coverless like a large
cup or graduated scale.[b] This receptacle is described by
Chrétien as being of solid gold, set with the most precious
stones, and giving forth a light so intense as to exceed
by far that of the candelabra that illuminate the hall
(ll. 3220 f.). This is the only attribute ascribed to the
mysterious object when it first appears in the procession
to which it gives its name. It is only much later (ll. 6420 f.)
that Perceval learns from his uncle, the holy hermit, that
in spite of its connection with the Fisher King the
receptacle did not contain 'pike, lampreys, and salmon',
but a single host which served to nourish, not the king or
his court, but the flesh and spirit of his old father, never
before mentioned in the poem: *Tant sainte chose est li
graaus.*[c]

It is, of course, possible that the poet deliberately waited
until he had reached line 6425 to reveal this fact in order
to keep his reader or listener in suspense—a common
device in chivalric romances of all ages. However, the fact
remains that in the context of the story, the phrase *sainte
chose* is totally incomprehensible, if we take it in the
normal Christian sense, that is to say, if the *sainte chose*
(referring to the Grail that contains a host) designates the
Eucharist as established and defined in the greatest sacra-
ment of the Catholic Church. We must therefore ask the

question: did the receptacle contain a liturgically consecrated host, or not? If the answer is in the affirmative,
then the whole of that ceremony of which it forms the
centre would appear even more blasphemous and incon-
ceivable from a Christian poet's point of view. On the
other hand, if it has not been consecrated, why is the Grail
tant sainte chose, and why does the host possess such supernatural virtue that it can provide physical and spiritual
sustenance for an old sovereign who has spent the past
fifteen years confined to his castle, in the company of these
symbolic objects?[1]

Such, then, is the dilemma from which there seems to
be no escape, least of all in the nebulous region of Celtic
folklore or in pagan literature, or in exotic texts of ancient
or medieval times, or in the biblical tradition.[a] Neither
may we seek the solution to so many mysteries in the
traditions of the Byzantine Mass, which may well have
served as a point of departure or a model for the various
objects borne in the procession, but which cannot have
inspired their role and function in the poem.[2] What, then,

[1] Some versions of the poem have 'doze ans' instead of fifteen (cf. ed.
A. Hilka, l. 6429) while two others have 'xi anz'. However, these
divergences do not affect the meaning of the episode.

[2] Mario Roques rightly points out in his preface to the translation by
L. Foulet of the *Conte del Graal*, Paris, 1947, pp. xxv f., that in both the
Greek and Roman rites the sacred objects (candles, chalices, patens, and
so forth) or the Byzantine knife used to cut the consecrated bread
(known as the 'lancea Christi') are always borne in procession by priests
and accompanied by a crucifix, which, as we have seen, is not the case
in this episode of Chrétien's poem. This deprives it of any liturgical or
Christian significance. M. Roques (p. xxiii) concludes that the Grail is
a sacred receptacle but not a divine relic or mystical vessel as it appears
in the later romances of the Arthurian cycle.

is the purpose of the silver 'tailleor' that follows the Grail in this procession, and of which no further mention is made in the whole of the rest of the poem? Whereas a single host suffices to nourish a man for the whole of his life, an empty paten accompanying the Grail with such pomp and circumstance would seem to have no purpose whatever. Having arrived at such a formidable *non liquet*, we must resign ourselves to the conclusion that such numerous and obvious internal contradictions will never provide us with a solution that will satisfy either the logic or the poetry of the tale. Admittedly, one of the experts has recently put forward the supposition that it is the Grail that sanctifies the host, and not the other way round.[1] But this only means that its consecration at no time occurs in a liturgical, Christian sense. Nor can this consecration be replaced by pagan magic, since the sanctity of the 'Grail' is, as we have seen, proclaimed by a pious hermit who leads Perceval to the true faith and orthodox religious practice.[2] Even fiction has its own logic, which would be totally absent here if we insisted on interpreting the mysterious objects of the procession as Eucharistic symbols for a sacrilegious travesty of the Communion service.

[1] Cf. P. Imbs, 'Perceval et le Graal chez Chrétien de Troyes', *Bulletin de la Société Académique du Bas-Rhin*, LXXII–LXXIV, 1950–52, pp. 71 f., whose interpretation is accepted with some reservations by Jean Frappier in 'Le Graal et l'Hostie', *Colloques, etc.*, pp. 63 f.

[2] Here, for the first time, in a 'chapele petite' (l. 6342) Perceval attends a Catholic service, conducted by a priest and a clerk, and confesses his sins before beginning his act of penance and obtaining advice to help him lead a truly Christian life. This episode includes ll. 6342–513 and is in some respects the most prominent in the whole poem.

It would, moreover, have been impossible for Chrétien himself to treat the matter so lightly. No matter how pious his intentions may have been, he could not have 'played' with the Eucharist and made it a 'deus ex machina' in a chivalric romance at a time when Eucharistic debates (which only ceased after the miracle of Bolsena in 1263) were exceedingly keen and troubled both laymen and priests, sceptics and believers, in the France of the 'Vaudois' and numerous other heretical sects. These sects differed widely in their theological beliefs and methods of worship, but placed at the very centre of their metaphysical speculations the problem of the relationship between matter and spirit, sin and redemption.

*   *   *

According to the hermit's account, it is not the Fisher King that draws physical and spiritual nourishment from the host within the Grail, but the king's father. This fleeting figure without a name or any other distinguishing characteristic had been for the past fifteen years a prisoner in the castle, in a room adjoining the hall where the banquet of the king, his son, takes place before the astonished eyes of Perceval, the latter's guest and nephew.[a] It is this contrast that Chrétien wished to emphasize, by opposing this man who feeds upon a purely spiritual nourishment to those who can take delight in the most tasty dishes.[1] The *esperitaus* in the castle is a man who, in his retreat, has reached the height of spiritual perfection by living on the host contained in the precious luminous

[1] These are enumerated in ll. 3280 f. and 3312-33.

vessel which, together with the other symbolic objects, makes its appearance before the guests at the banquet and those who serve them according to court ceremonial.

While the hermit, who is related to him, lives in the solitude of a wood and practises abstinence and the rites of the Christian religion, the mysterious personage in the castle seems to personify the ideal figure of those who desire to attain superhuman perfection without the aid of the liturgy and ecclesiastical guidance, like the 'perfect ones' of the new sects, who were venerated in France by the faithful and respected even by Catholics for their holy life of absolute abstinence, completely dedicated to the elimination of the last dross of matter, of evil and sin.[a] The host of the Grail cannot be the 'Corpus Christi' consecrated in the Catholic Mass. Hence it is the Grail, and not a liturgical act, that consecrates the host and confers miraculous powers upon it to the extent of affording physical and spiritual nourishment to a penitent ascetic. But through what virtue can this have occurred, according to our poet's fiction? Certainly not because the Grail was made of precious metal, for according to a lengthy tradition and the decrees of various synods (including the one held at Rouen in 1189), all chalices, ciboria, and patens had to be of either gold or silver, except in the poorest churches.[1] And here we are at the court of the 'Riche roi Pescheor', who, although he is an invalid, keeps up all the appearances due to his state. Nor could this virtue have proceeded from the precious stones, even *des plus riches et des plus chieres* (l. 3236), even though, as is well known, medieval lapidaries attributed great powers

[1] Joseph Braun, *Das Christliche Altargerät*, p. 38 f.

to them.[1] Their function in church usage had been defined in the year 1145 by the Abbot Suger of Saint-Denis whom the contemplation of these precious ornaments had led to ponder the *sanctarum diversitatem virtutum* and transfer it, *anagogico more*, to the celestial spheres of creation.[2]

And since no one can still give serious credence to the idea that the magic cauldron of the Celts had evolved to the point of becoming the object described by Chrétien in his poem,[3] we are left with the hypothesis, not to say the certainty—that it is the intense light given forth by the Grail that accomplishes the miracle, sanctifying the receptacle and consecrating the host therein contained. In Robert de Boron's *Estoire*, in which the Grail has become the depository for the sacred blood of Christ, we likewise find that it sends forth *la grant clarté* that miraculously illuminates the prison of Joseph of Arimathea, its custodian, with no attribute or ornament other than its own splendour. *Sires Diex toupuissanz*, the author asks, *dont vient ceste clatrez si granz?*[4] In a poem such as Robert's, inspired by evangelical sentiments and episodes, it is easy to recognize in the light of the Grail the *lux mundi* with which Jesus identified himself, according to St John's Gospel (8: 2), saying that *qui sequitur me non ambulat in tenebris, sed habebit lumen vitae*. This is indeed one of the

[1] For French lapidaries of the Middle Ages, cf. Ch. V. Langlois, *La Connaissance de la nature et du monde au Moyen Age, etc.*, Paris, 1927.

[2] For the text, with English translation and notes, cf. E. Panofsky, *Abbot Suger*, Princeton, N. J., 1946, pp. 62, 183. For such ornamentation of sacred objects in the Middle Ages, see J. Braun, op. cit., pp. 146 f., 233 f., and 337.

[3] On this point it is possible to agree with Mme Lot-Borodine, *Romania*, LXXVII, p. 234.   [4] Ed. cit., ll. 727–9.

metaphors for which the Evangelist had a characteristic preference that distinguishes him from the Synoptics, who were less given to the use of allegory and figurative language. Moreover, its influence is not limited to Robert: it extends to medieval mystical theology inspired by the emanationist doctrines of that Gnostic and Alexandrian philosophy, consecrated by St Augustine and handed down by the Arabs, which came to assert itself in the twelfth century as the dominant tendency of pre- and anti-Scholastic Christian thought.[a]

But this imagery, meaningful though it is in Robert's poem, would make little sense in the wholly profane setting of the Fisher King's castle with its systematic distortion of the most sacred rites of the Byzantine and Roman Churches. We may therefore wonder why none of the ingenious interpreters of this episode in the *Conte del Graal* has ever thought of repeating Joseph of Arimathea's question, and why they have consistently ignored the one feature—the light that streams from the vessel—that distinguishes the Grail from every other liturgical object, none of which, incidentally, is to be found in the hall of the enchanted castle. It is no less surprising to find that no mention of this wonderful light occurs in the 500 pages dedicated to the Grail with immense, yet unavailing, learning by Konrad Burdach, or that the late E. Hoepffner, usually so penetrating and precise in his studies on the subject, should have accorded no importance to this element, and considered it an insignificant minutia.[1]

It would not be difficult to discover in the resplendent light of Chrétien's Grail the *Lumen Christi* of Christian

[1] Cf. *Colloques, etc.*, p. 96.

liturgy, which was invoked in private and ecclesiastical worship from the time of the earliest communities. These perpetuated, with different intentions, pagan mysteries and cults centring upon the sun and its light in the sacred rites of bread and wine or in the agape.[1] But the omission of any liturgical act accompanying the invocation and the brief ceremony (still practised today), and the total absence of symbols indicating the power of the Church (a crown or halo) on the head of the damsel who carries the Grail lead us to suspect a heterodox or heretical meaning in this unusual holy light which would exclude any manifestation of traditional Catholic worship.

It is precisely this 'gralophorous' maiden who provides us with the necessary proof. Authentic documents and authorities regarding the religious history of the time tell us that, among the heretical groups in Flanders, Champagne, Brittany and, later, Provence and Italy, certain women who shared in the supposed divinity of their leaders, such as the celebrated Tanchelm of Antwerp and Éon de l'Étoile, embodied this Godhead under the name of *Sapientia* (which had replaced the more ancient *Sophia* or *Gnosis*), signifying supreme knowledge and enlightened wisdom; or *Maria*, a celestial personage who has nothing whatever in common with her Christian namesake, just as their Jesus is not to be identified with the crucified Saviour and Christ of the Gospels.[a] It would therefore seem that the light-bearing figure in the poem is in fact one of those mystical women who made their appearance

[1] Cf. F. J. Dölger's exhaustive study, *Antike und Christentum*, 1936, vol. v, pp. 1–43.

in the heretical movements of the age, and who must have been well known to contemporary readers for the part these movements played in the dramatic public happenings instigated by fanatical agitators and their followers, ready in their ecstasy to face horrible torture and even death at the stake, unperturbed if not smiling.

Anyone who is unacquainted with the religious fervour, sectarian violence, mystical excesses, and bizarre symbolism of those heretical communities will undoubtedly consider our interpretation far-fetched. Chrétien de Troyes, writing for an audience of princes and lords, has placed in a regal setting the secret rites, esoteric symbols, and visionary sentiments of those who, beneath Christian appearances, shared in the religious aberrations of his age.[a] This ambiguity of terms and rites, which so irritated the inquisitors and which made the sectarians appear even more blasphemous, was a general—even universal— aspect of the heretical sects that belonged to the Gnostic and Manichaean tradition. The former went back to the age of St Paul,[1] while the latter originated with the teachings of Mani, who had pushed to its extreme consequences the dualism of the transcendent god of light and the god of darkness, creator and ruler of the material world, thereby initiating the cult of the cosmic and incorporeal *Jesus patibilis*.[2] In Chrétien's time, and even

[1] Cf. G. Bornkamm, *Paulusstudien*, 1952; W. Schmithals, *Die Gnosis in Korinth*, Göttingen, 1956, and preceding works quoted in these recent studies. Also Hans Jonas, *The Gnostic Religion*, Boston, 1958; R. M. Grant, *Gnosticism and Early Christianity*, New York, 1959, esp. p. 150 f.; and R. Bultmann, *Gnosis*, London, 1952, p. 41 f., all fully documented.

[2] Cf. H. Ch. Puech, *Le Manichéisme*, esp. p. 82 f., and the extensive notes.

before, this cult had in the West replaced the phantas-
magoria of Manichaean mythology and had developed
doctrines and practices that were Christian in appearance
but Gnostic or at least heterodox in substance.[a]

Such sects were dominated by the concept expressed by
St John the Evangelist at the beginning of his first epistle:
Deus est lux, et tenebrae in eo non sunt ullae.[b] This is the light
of the Grail. Only those penitents who, by the practice of
extreme abstinence and chastity, had freed themselves
from the last remnants of dark matter and thereby re-
gained their original angelic nature might return to it.
The co-existence of spirit and matter in the consecrated
Eucharist was just as unthinkable for them as that of good
and evil, light and darkness, redemption and sin. The
mystery of the Grail and its host, unfathomable from the
Catholic point of view, may be explained by placing it in
the setting of these doctrines that were known and understood by so many of our poet's contemporaries, even
though Chrétien himself never adhered to them. The
effulgent receptacle's sole purpose is to bring to the penitent the nourishment sanctified by the light with which
the good and transcendent god is identified and through
which he reveals himself to the elect. It is a heterodox
symbol, sacred, but not liturgical, and as such belongs
to a ritual vaguely connected with the traditions of
Christian worship, yet with a profoundly different meaning. The host contained in the Grail signifies something
quite different from the Eucharist of Catholic worship,
which in the twelfth century was itself still an object of
theological debate and widespread doubt concerning the
concepts of the 'corpus verum' and 'corpus mysticum' of

the 'impanatio' and 'transubstantiatio': all of which were resolved only after a great deal of controversy by the Lateran Council of 1215, and, more particularly, by the great Scholastics that succeeded it.[1]

Chrétien's host brings to mind the consecrated bread that was broken and distributed to the faithful in the sacramental banquets that constituted the sole ceremony normally celebrated by Catharist communities. It was unaccompanied by any priest, altar, or any other rite, while the transcendent Jesus was invoked as the mediator between the god of light and sinful humanity governed by the devil, the god of darkness and lord of the material world. This was the so-called 'supersubstantial bread', only apparently related to the historical Jesus and quite different from the 'corpus Christi' of Catholic worship. It was mentioned, in place of the 'daily bread' of Christian liturgy, in the *Pater Noster*, the only prayer recited at the sacramental banquets of Catharist–Manichaean tradition.[a]

As for the 'tailleor' that follows the Grail in the procession at the Castle and inexplicably makes its appearance at the subsequent banquet, it recalls the dish that bore the symbolic bread distributed to the faithful in their sole Sunday rite when they invoked the incorporeal Jesus of their faith. All their churches, except those of the most radical Albigensians, had kept this symbolic act, although they did not admit that *ex illo pane conficiatur corpus Christi*.[b] A certain degree of sanctity, however heterodox, could be attributed to this 'supersubstantial bread'.

[1] For this complex and difficult subject, see H. de Lubac, *Corpus Mysticum*, 2nd. ed., Paris, 1949, and the comprehensive articles in the *Dictionnaire de Théologie Catholique*.

Bérenger de Tours (d. 1088) had proclaimed, within the supposed bounds of Catholic orthodoxy, that although the bread blessed by Christ and the host of his cult were a mere 'signum' they were as sacred as a liturgically consecrated host.[a] In spite of various condemnations and Bérenger's recantation at the synod of Rome in 1059, this thesis, which was famous in the age of Abélard and St Bernard, fired the unceasing Eucharistic debates of the Middle Ages and remained with the heretics as their sole concession to Christian tradition, which was otherwise rejected in all its doctrinal and liturgical aspects.[1] The numerous churchmen and laymen who were then troubled by doubts regarding the Eucharistic doctrine understood and in part recognized this distinction which appeared to them as an acceptable compromise. The host contained in the Grail—the supersubstantial bread—nourishes the King who

> est si esperitaus
> qu'a sa vie plus ne covient.
> (ll. 6427–8)

It does so independently of all liturgy and through a mystical power of its own. And the hermit could in this sense assert the sanctity of the Grail and its host, without blasphemous contradiction, and thereby succeed in placing the remission of Perceval's sins and his subsequent communion in direct opposition to the way of life practised by the inhabitants of the Castle, who evidently managed without either of these sacraments.

It is important to observe the manner in which this

[1] *Liber de duobus principiis, etc.*, ed. A. Dondaine, p. 47.

final absolution takes place, after the rite celebrated in the chapel. The hermit is not a churchman or a canonically ordained person; he is a penitent layman, like his equivalent Trevrizent in a scene from Wolfram von Eschenbach's *Parzifal*, which is far more elaborate and yet substantially identical (although the German poet refers to the problematic Kyōt and the mysterious Flegetānis, a pagan astrologer).[1] We are not obliged to consider him, or his French prototype, a heretic or heterodox dissenter; nor must we equate the two ceremonies of absolution with the *consolamentum* of the Catharists.[2] For in neither poem do we find the laying on of hands of the 'Perfect', who serves as a paraclete or 'comforter', a kind of spiritual baptism conferred upon the head of the believer after difficult and lengthy trials, and after a reading of the prologue to St John's Gospel (1: 9), in which the *lux vera quae illuminat omnem hominem venientem in hunc mundum* is opposed to the darkness of matter.[3]

---

[1] Lib. IX, 453, 11 f. This is one of the best known and most controversial passages in this long poem. It presents the mysteries of the Grail in a way that is quite different from Chrétien's. Flegetānis is, of course, the title of an Arab text, *Felek-thâni*. Trevrizent is explicitly called 'ein leic' (ibid., 462, 11) and such is certainly the hermit in the *Conte del Graal*.

[2] This is the conclusion arrived at by E. H. Zeydel, 'Wolframs Parzifal, Kyot und die Katharer', *Neophilologus*, XXXVII, 1953, p. 28 f., accepted in part by Wapnewski, *Wolframs Parzival, etc.*, p. 176 f., and supported and developed by others. For discussions of the German problem, cf. H. J. Koppitz, *Wolframs Religiosität*, dissertation, Bonn, 1958, p. 305 f. These works help to interpret obscure points in the corresponding episode in Chrétien's poem.

[3] Cf. A. Borst, *Die Katharer*, Stuttgart, 1953, p. 192 f.; A. Dondaine, op. cit., p. 34 f.

In Chrétien's poem Perceval, together with his uncle
the hermit, devoutly listens to Mass served by a priest and
a clerk, on Good Friday, in the hermitage chapel. Afterwards, his uncle instructs him in the Christian faith. This
instruction, however, is far removed even from the
canonical usage of those times. The hermit whispers a
prayer in which the name of God recurs frequently, and
Perceval is told that he should utter this name only in case
of extreme danger or on the point of death.[1] The Church
has never known such an ineffable prayer or this method
of teaching it to converts or the faithful. It is true that
after two days of devout penance Perceval acknowledges
that God died on the cross—as the poet has it—on a
Friday, and obtained the grace of Communion on Easter
Day.[2] But in spite of this the procedure has more than one
illegitimate aspect, and may be taken as the first literary
proof of the extent to which the ordinances and rites of
Catholic worship could at that time be imprecise, change-
able, and even arbitrary, and yet remain valid and free
from the charge of heresy. While the debates of the

[1] ll. 6481–92.

[2]
> Aprés le servise aora
> La croiz et ses pechiez plora . . .
> Einsi Percevaus reconut
> Que Deus au vandredi reçut
> Mort et si fu crocefiiez.
> A la pasque comeniiez
> Fu Percevaus mout dignemant.
> (ll. 6495–513)

Without going into details, Mario Roques quite simply asserts that this
communion is 'hors de l'usage régulier de l'Église' (preface to E.
Foulet's translation, p. xxvi).

theologians (such as Abélard, Peter Lombard, St Anselm, Hugo of Saint Victor, and others) waxed hot on this point, lay confession and absolution were fairly frequent and apparently legitimized by the widespread belief that remission of sins could occur before absolution, when, as in Perceval's case, contrition was sincere, total, and accompanied by the desire to obtain these graces from one who was appointed to impart them, or worthy of so doing.[1]

Chrétien does not specify whether his hero received Holy Communion for the first time in his life from an ordained priest, in the hermit's chapel, or from this same lay penitent to whom, as we are told, other lay folk, knights, and ladies had confessed their sins and asked, on the same day, counsel for their salvation.[2] This, too, was not excluded from Catholic usage of the times, and was obviously practised by many who adhered to heterodox or heretical doctrines, or to rites that were considered Christian but were certainly not canonical. It was only in the year 1215, when Chrétien had been dead for some thirty years and Wolfram had already concluded his poem, that the Lateran Council, in order to eradicate these widespread errors decreed *hoc utique sacramentum nemo potest conficere nisi sacerdos qui fuerit rite ordinatus*.[3]

The hermit in the poem is not merely the prototype of

[1] See the comprehensive treatment of this subject in the *Dictionnaire de Théologie Catholique*, 1935, I, part I, col. 168–75.

[2] ll. 6217 f., and esp. 6301 f.

[3] Cf. the passage quoted by C. Mirbt, *Quellen zur Geschichte des Papstums,etc.*, p. 179 n. 329, and the entire text in the *Dictionnaire de Théol. Cath.*, loc. cit., col. 684.

many others that recur in chivalric romances, in both prose and verse, down to Ariosto; he is also a poetically true representative of those holy men who, in Chrétien's time and even in the preceding century, fled from the world and turned aside from religious communities in order to dedicate themselves as individuals to the salvation of their souls and the comfort of those who had recourse to them.[a] The hermit in Chrétien's romance, the son of the sovereign who feeds upon the host in the Grail and brother of the invalid Fisher King, is, in contrast to these persons, the one who has found the way of salvation by remaining within the true faith, to which he causes Perceval to return, while the magic castle of the others disappears forever, as a symbol of that illusion and error which the young hero, now redeemed, definitely renounces:

> De Perceval plus longuemant
> Ne parole li contes ci.
> (ll. 6514-15)

Such would appear to be, in accordance with the spirit of the times, the basic allegory of Chrétien's poem, which his continuators and imitators were soon to falsify by making it into a kind of 'conte dévot', like Robert de Boron's *Estoire*, or a complex romance of adventure with a happy ending, like Wolfram von Eschenbach's *Parzifal*.

*   *   *

In the Fisher King's castle the bleeding lance, the luminous vessel and the silver platter are all mere appearances which have no practical role to play and are not used for any form of worship. Instead, they appear as objects destined to arouse the curiosity of an inexperienced young man who has not the slightest knowledge of liturgy and is already marked by involuntary sin. The poet is constantly harping on these two aspects of his personality. If Perceval had but asked the reason for these mysterious objects and the ceremonial whereby they were presented, his conscience would have been roused, his soul saved, and the maimed Fisher King restored to health.' He ought to have asked the question put by Joseph of Arimathea in Robert de Boron's poem: *Dont vient ceste clartez si granz?* The reply would have illuminated the young adventurer and, in some mysterious way, broken the spell and brought back all the actors in the scene to truth and salvation.

However, Perceval is a predestined sinner who remains an onlooker before an outward show of worship. He does not pierce the mystery, which vainly continues to excite his curiosity until, just before the remission of his sins, his hermit uncle offers him an explanation. He asserts that Perceval's silence in the presence of so great a mystery was due not only to the advice of his tutor Gornemant not to talk too much or ask too many questions, but also to the fact that 'sin bound his tongue'.² The

---

¹ He is severely reproached for his careless indifference by his cousin, the 'pucele' (l. 3583 f.), and then violently rebuked by a mysterious woman of monstrous ugliness at Arthur's court (ll. 4646–83).

² *Pechiez la langue te trancha* (l. 6409), as the wise hermit tells him, who is more judicious than the ignorant woman who indignantly reproached him for his errors.

one to suffer from this silence is the invalid sovereign who guards those symbols. In this way, our interest is now diverted from the objects themselves towards the persons to whom they are presented.

The motivation of Perceval's behaviour is clear and coherent. We may see in him a symbolic figure of obvious significance. The Fisher King is a more mysterious character, represented in a vague, static manner. Together with his old father, he disappears before long from the action of the poem. Immobilized by his painful wound, he waits to be cured, in soul as well as in body, by a question which Perceval, prevented by his inhibitions, does not dare to ask. We shall never know for certain what form this liberating question took in the poet's imagination, except that it must obviously have had something to do with the reason for the king's infirmity and the spectacle Perceval had seen. Since a question demands or presupposes a reply, it could not have been intended to act like the magic word in folk-tales, but rather as something to induce a confession that would have freed the invalid from his curse. A profession of faith that would then have revealed the doctrines or beliefs hidden behind those mysterious symbols.

The information that Perceval shortly afterwards obtains from his cousin, the *pucele*, on resuming his wanderings (ll. 3422 f.) concerns only concrete facts which do not offer any key to so many enigmatic apparitions. She tells him that the invalid king had been struck by a javelin (*javelot*) in battle *parmi les hanches anbedeus*[a] and so maimed that he could no longer ride a horse or exercise his power. The fact that he indulges in fishing for a pastime explains his name 'the Fisher King' and little else:

> Et vet peschant a l'ameçon:
> Por ce li rois Peschierre a non.
>
> (ll. 3519–20)

This is clearly a rational explanation of his infirmity through an accident of war that could have happened to any warrior in those times, when—in fact as well as in fiction—the limbs of warriors were exposed, in spite of their armour, to the most horrible wounds and injuries. Moreover, the allusion to the wound *parmi les hanches anbedeus* is in fact a repetition of what Perceval's mother had told him just before their separation:

> Vostre pere, si nel savez,
> Fu parmi les janbes navrez
> Si que il maheigna del cors.
>
> (ll. 435–7)

The rationalization of the episode goes no further. The bleeding lance is isolated from the javelin that caused the incurable wound: it is presented as an object of purely symbolical value completely unrelated to the Fisher King's person.

What, then, is the nature of the wound that no medicine, but only a question put by Perceval, could have cured? This wound is not on the invalid's right side, like that inflicted upon Christ by Longinus.[1] It is, in fact—as

---

[1] For the representation of this wound in medieval painting and sculpture and in later art cf. Vladimir Gurewich, 'Observations

we see from the euphemism used by the poet—nothing less than emasculation. It is designated as such in explicit terms by Wolfram von Eschenbach, who thus gives us the interpretation current in his day.[a] Before the total Christianization of the Grail saga, which began shortly afterwards with Robert de Boron (who does not mention the bleeding lance), the association of the wound with Christ's Passion would have appeared unthinkably blasphemous, totally unrelated to the terrible mutilation which prevents the Fisher King from moving, reigning, or perpetuating his dynasty.[b] It represents a curse that hangs over Perceval's family. His unhappy mother, having vaguely discerned it, tries in vain to prevent her one surviving son from setting forth on the road to chivalric adventure. And yet both of the protagonists in this dramatic account must be healed and saved; the invalid king from his fatal wound, the young knight from his foolish errors; the knight through conversion to the true faith, the king by means of a question that is never expressed.

Like everything else that concerns the king, his mutilation and his prolonged martyrdom have a symbolic value, and as such must refer to the cause of man's damnation.[c] He is injured in his virility which lies at the root of all sin. Not that Chrétien, who was a poet and not a moralist, had to make any specific pronouncement on this point. The idea of sin and redemption was at the ideological core of the whole of his epic. Perceval is frequently rebuked for his sins, which, since they are quite

on the Iconography of the Wound in Christ's Side, etc.', *Journal of the Warburg and Courtauld Institutes*, XX, 1957, pp. 358–62.

involuntary, represent a fatal influence on the sinner rather than any evil will on his part.[1] Nor would the medieval reader or listener have missed the double meaning evident in the name of this ruler who is the victim of a hidden destiny. The Old French *pescheor* and *pecheor* were homonyms, derived from the Latin *piscatore* (*m*) and *peccatore* (*m*) respectively. In modern French *pêcheur* and *pécheur* are distinguished only by the accent; in written Old French, by the preservation of *s* in the consonant group *sch* (*stš*). This *s*, however, was no longer distinctly pronounced in Chrétien's day.[2] The poet himself emphasizes this homonymy (puns were popular among the educated classes of those times) in the dramatic episode that concludes Perceval's conversion. His uncle the hermit tells him:

> Et prie Deu que merci et
> De l'ame de son pecheor;

whereupon he replies:

> Sire, chiés le Roi Pescheor
> Fui une foiz . . .
> (ll. 6370-2)

---

[1] A distinction exhaustively discussed by St Augustine and taken up again by theologians and moralists of the twelfth century, as shown in Wapnewski's succinct account, loc. cit. and p. 109 f. It is particularly true in the case of the maimed king, although it is also valid for Perceval, except for the innocent romantic adventure referred to on p. 7 above.

[2] For this linguistic phenomenon see the concise account in E. Bourciez, *Éléments de Linguistique Romane* (deuxième édition), Paris, 1923, §273.

Linked by rhyme, the two significant terms become fused in a single concept.[1] Is it not likely, then, that in creating the character of the Fisher King—or the Sinner King—Chrétien was inspired by the double meaning of the word, and that this ambiguity points to the allegorical message of the romance as a whole?[2] This is no more than a possibility, but anyone who is acquainted with the mentality of the age will find it difficult to believe that the meaning of the pun did not reveal itself spontaneously to the poet's contemporaries, for whom all names were the consequence of things.[a] Such an explanation of the king's innocent pastime would have the further advantage of removing any link, such as has been suggested by some authoritative modern interpreters of the story, between this pastime and the symbolic monogram of Christ ($I\chi\theta\upsilon\varsigma$)—a *rapprochement* which would have been considered sacrilegious by Chrétien's contemporaries.[b]

The maimed king and the young knight are, then, the two living symbols of a sin that is not caused by their will or by any perversion, but by a destiny that persecutes them. Neither the king nor the knight ever seems to have been guilty of incontinence or concupiscence, or to have

[1] This is a common device in medieval literature, both Latin and vernacular, and it is even found in scientific and philosophical writings. In Robert de Boron's *Estoire dou Graal* (ed. Nitze, ll. 2659-61), a fictitious Petrus explains the meaning of the term 'Graal' by stating that 'nus le Graal ne verra, ce croie je, qu'il ne li *agree*', and insisting (l. 2663) that 'a touz agree et abelist', as if the sacred receptacle had been given this name because it was 'agréable'. Helinand (see p. 15 above) has 'graalz quia grata et acceptabilis'.

[2] This is certainly the way in which Wolfram interpreted Chrétien's intentions. He transformed the French poet's discreet allusions into an explicit symbol of the sin of love.

sinned against the rules of chivalry, which demanded courage, loyalty, honour, and the protection of ladies and the weak.[a] Chrétien does not specify the nature of the sin in either case, leaving it to the reader to guess what it was. Was it Perceval's fault that he unwittingly brought about his mother's death? Or the invalid king's that he was the victim of original sin, as it would seem? In both cases we are confronted with a sin *sine malitia*, a type of sin much debated by contemporary Catholic theologians and attributed by heretics to the evil demon's power over men.[b] And yet, both must endure their suffering—the one moral, the other physical—until the time of their redemption.

Perceval's conversion is known, but the unfinished romance does not tell us how the poet had conceived that of the maimed king. Robert de Boron begins the Christianization of the story by addressing in the first verse of his *Estoire dou Graal*

Tout pecheeur,
Et li petit et li meneur.

This naïve and pedestrian poem, completely lacking in the psychological *finesse* and epic inspiration of Chrétien's *Conte*,[c] is nevertheless based on the same moral concepts: the intentions are similar, although the story is presented in a totally different spirit and setting—and in spite of the fact that Robert attempted to connect his evangelical, Eucharistic tale with the Arthurian tradition by mentioning at the end of his poem the Vale of Avalon with its echoes of historical and sacred happenings that were supposed to have taken place in the kingdom of

England.[1] The similarity of his moral purpose with Chrétien's is borne out by the fact that, among other things, in Robert's poem Joseph of Arimathea, the guardian of the Grail, and his group of Christian followers are stricken with infirmity *pour le pechié de luxure* (l. 2383), until the sacred vessel (now the chalice in which the blood of Christ was collected) brings to light the true sinners and allows the elect to attain to the grace of God.[2] Here the pun on the words *pêcheur* and *pécheur*—more precisely, *peschiere* and *pechiere*—is found with even more obvious apologetic implications. In the same episode, Hebron (or Bron), Joseph of Arimathea's brother-in-law, is asked to catch a fish and place it, together with the Grail, on the table which serves as an altar, so as to give a symbolic imitation of the Last Supper and bring about the miracle of the separation of the sinners from those who are definitely saved.[a] Whereupon this obscure character with a Biblical name is transformed by Robert into a 'Riche Pêcheur', obviously inspired by Chrétien's Fisher King, while the latter's royal station and courtly entourage are replaced by a Eucharistic symbol that corresponds to his devout intentions.[3]

What we have here is a completely orthodox treatment and transformation of the ambiguous religious and moral elements in Chrétien's poem, all of which must have been well known to the pious author of the *Estoire*. What seems sacrilegious in the one is devotion in the other; and,

[1] Cf. ll. 3123 and 3220.

[2] ll. 2555–638.

[3] Hebron assumes the title and name of 'Riche Pescheeur' (l. 3345) or 'Riches Peschierres', etc., after he has become—like Chrétien's Fisher King—the custodian of the Grail.

whereas the insistence on the idea of sin and final redemption creates a bond between them, it is clear that Robert wished to make a deliberate contrast between the heterodox or frankly heretical implications in the *Conte* and the gospel or apocryphal reminiscences that serve as didactic themes in his edifying and entirely orthodox poem.[1] Later, in the prose version of the Quest of the Grail, such reminiscences are made to conform more and more to the ascetic ideals of monastic life, linked with the chivalric tradition inaugurated by the *Conte del Graal* of Chrétien de Troyes.[2]

The obsession with sin, expiation, and redemption, which inspires and animates the whole of this literature beneath the surface of its adventurous fancies, is evident in the very first examples of it that have come down to us. It is an obsession highly symptomatic of its age, when these concepts were being debated to the point of exasperation between orthodox believers and heretics intent on bringing about a total renovation of religious life and ethics. The concept of sin as a metaphysical necessity was then proclaimed, together with the denial of free will, by the sects, groups, and reformers who upheld, in conformity with Gnostic and Manichaean traditions, the co-eternity of good and evil, and thus provoked the Catholic reaction which, from St Bernard to St Dominic,

[1] For the sources of the *Estoire*, cf. W. A. Nitze, ed. cit., introduction, p. 9 f., and E. Hoepffner, op. cit., p. 96.

[2] Cf. the various studies by A. Pauphilet, which are now partly gathered together (with a bibliography of his writings) in *Le Legs du Moyen Age*, Melun, 1950, esp. pp. 170 f., 212 f.; also the articles published in *Colloques, etc.* and others mentioned in F. W. Locke's informative book, *The Quest for the Holy Grail, etc.*, Stanford, Calif., 1960.

D

restored to the Christian sacraments the power of redeem-
ing man from his sins.[a]

The lance that never stops bleeding (l. 6410) is therefore, like St Augustine's *telum*, a symbol of evil, which is
eternal even as good is eternal. It thereby represents one
of the two cosmic principles on which the heterodox
theology and morality of Chrétien's contemporaries were
based, in dialectical contrast with the Christian doctrines
of sin and redemption. The other principle is embodied in
the dazzling light of the Grail, which is very different
from the magic bowls found in fables or even the famous
pātra of Buddha, which, Marco Polo tells us, was of fine
green porphyry and so made that 'by placing in it enough
food for one, it was possible to feed five persons'.[b]
Chrétien's Grail unlike that in Wolfram von Eschenbach's
poem does not supply the numerous dainty dishes which
the poet takes delight in describing at the castle banquet
(ll. 3280–335). It appears exclusively as a source of symbolic light in the way described above, a fact which meant
much more to Chrétien's contemporaries than it does to
modern interpreters of the poem. The notion of light
being consubstantial with the Godhead, and not a simple
metaphor, had been accepted—in accordance with
Gnostic, Paulician, and Manichaean traditions—by numberless religious communities in France and Provence, as
well as in Italy and Germany. There are, moreover, two
significant omissions. First, in an episode that is evidently
soteriological in character, we find no cross, altar, or
churchman in the castle. Secondly, in the age of St Bernard, when the cult of the Virgin had reached its highest
point in theology and its most splendid expression in art,

we do not find any trace of it in a poem that is supposed to be completely and devoutly orthodox. Indeed, it is only just before his confession and absolution that Perceval for the first time hears mention made *de la Virge dame* and of the Incarnation, from the lips of his uncle the hermit.[1]

All this reveals the influence of the teachings and practices of those superficially Christian cults, heretical and even pagan in inspiration, which, while keeping alive the concept of redemption and the transcendent image of Christ, had abolished every form of church worship, the Eucharist, the sign of the cross—everything that could recall the Saviour's real humanity—suppressed the sacraments, such as baptism and marriage, and made their 'perfect' members practise the most extreme forms of abstinence and asceticism, in which the ordinary 'believers' were instructed, though they were not required to apply them.[2] We thus find in the poem two contrasting manifestations of purificatory penance: on the one hand, the ascetic who lives on an unconsecrated host in surroundings completely lacking in any ecclesiastical feature or sacred ritual; on the other, the hermit who looks after his purification, admittedly on an individual basis, yet according to the teachings of the Roman Church which he imparts to the young knight, 'errant' both in behaviour and spirit;—a contrast that reveals the author's intentions and the meaning of his work.

All of this, which is found in veiled form in the castle scene and in the treatment of the characters, gives rise to

[1] l. 6264 f.
[2] Unlike Wolfram von Eschenbach in his *Parzifal*, Chrétien never mentions his heroes' wives.

misleading religious appearances. It is impossible to tell whether they are Christian or pagan, ecclesiastical or profane, modelled on existing liturgies or the work of the poet's imagination, since they partake of all these elements. The reason for the rejection of the basic forms of Catholic worship in all those heterodox and heretical sects was rooted in their common dualism, which maintained the incompatibility of matter (as the eternal manifestation of the force of evil) with the spirit of good, represented by the divinity of light. Without attempting to penetrate the labyrinth of the nebulous heretical theology resulting from these principles, we would merely remind the reader of the moral consequences of such a faith, which conceived human nature as a continuous struggle to eliminate every particle of cosmic evil from its necessary and fatal coexistence with good, in order to arrive at an angelic purity that allows the human soul to unite completely with the god of light. For the masters of this faith, human life is nothing but an expiation of that primordial sin when the genius of evil succeeded in corrupting man's angelic nature—an expiation that strives at freeing him from the bonds of matter and leading him back to his angelic perfection.

This, too, was as clear to contemporaries as it is obscure for us, especially if we vainly attempt to unravel the secrets of the Grail and its first romance by plunging into the unfathomable mysteries of a distant past or a misty folklore of uncertain origin and date. Chrétien has projected into the chivalric society with which he was familiar the religious problems and conflicts that troubled his contemporaries in more or less open contrast with the teachings, clergy, and institutions of the Catholic Church. The public debates, trials, ecclesiastical reaction, and intervention on the part of the political authorities in their attempt to prevent the spread of heretical doctrines and to suppress them by fire and sword, which culminated in the massacres at Albi and elsewhere, all placed these heretics at the centre of the spiritual, political, and moral interests of the times.

The French courts and the high clergy were well aware of this, while the secular arm assisted Catholic repression, when necessary, in executing the judgments of the bishops and great feudal lords.[a] We should remember that it was precisely in these years when Chrétien was engaged in the composition of his poem that his patron, Count Philip of Flanders, took part in the struggle against the heretics who had flourished in this province for many years past.[b] Rich merchants and especially the provincial nobility throughout France and the lands of Languedoc gave their ardent support to these movements, whose centres of expansion were to be found in Flanders and in Chrétien's own Champagne.[1] It is therefore highly probable that this prince, who was so active in this repression before joining the Third Crusade, charged the greatest courtly poet of his times with the composition of a poetic allegory for his fellow nobles. This allegory was of course to be placed in the familiar Arthurian setting. It was intended to delight

[1] This fact is well known and duly recorded in all the histories of French heretical movements, already quoted on several occasions, as well as the *Histoire de l'Église*, vol. IX, p. 335 f., and esp. A. Borst, *Die Katharer* (see the articles 'Champagne' and 'Flandern' in the *Namen-und-Sachregister*). A comprehensive study of the sociological background of this phenomenon would be most instructive.

its audience by means of the apologetic and moral intentions expressed in the prologue, which may already have
been set forth, in a form unknown to us, in the *livre* to
which the poet refers.[a]

It was no doubt from this source that Chrétien drew
the idea of writing a work of religious apology—an idea
that is completely lacking in all his previous poems—
whereas the romantic episodes were no doubt the product
of his poetic imagination alone. The Grail procession, its
various symbols and characters, the subtle psychological
insights which reveal profound human experience, both
of maternal and profane love (as, for example, the three
bloodstains on the freshly fallen snow which remind the
wandering hero of Blancheflor), all this and much besides
is pure poetry and not folklore or erudition; original
creation and not pedantic imitation.[b] Any attempt to
penetrate further into the secrets of a poet of passion and
feeling is vain curiosity rather than enlightened criticism.
We must be satisfied with an understanding of the inspiration and purpose of this work which is so different from
Chrétien's other poems; a work which has lost nothing of
its freshness throughout the ages and very little of its
moral and religious significance.

Although Chrétien left his romance unfinished, its *sen*
must have been obvious to contemporaries, who saw in
it a reflection of their destiny, their sufferings and aspirations. For them, the castle of the Grail cannot have been
the mere seat of a powerless ruler without any direct heir.
It must also have appeared the centre of a sect, or rather a
new order, distinguished from all others by its heterodox
organization.[c] Its mysteries were not revealed; neverthe-

less, they must have been fairly intelligible to a society that was troubled by Eucharistic problems, moral aspirations, and by the violent reactions against the pessimistic asceticism that flourished side by side with the refinements of court life, the splendour of church buildings, the rebirth of the schools, and the worldly leanings of the higher clergy.

Chrétien, as can be seen in all his poetic production, was a cultured man without professional pedantry, optimistic and lacking in dogmatic fanaticism. He was naturally attracted by the new courtly civilization which his heroes embodied, but interested as he was in all that went on around him, he was also a gifted story-teller, never frivolous or thoughtless. Like all his contemporaries, he could not conceive of poetry without its *sen*, which was a puzzle that subtle minds like his own set out to solve. The episode of the Grail shows us that he wished to bring into play, discreetly and yet with sufficient emphasis, the religious aberrations that menaced the orthodoxy of courtly society, not only in his own country but in the whole of contemporary Christian Europe.

In this he showed the same flair as in the characteristic spiritual manifestations of that society which formerly he had in part created and revealed in his worldly romances, before one of the greatest of French princes urged him on towards higher ideals. The total Christianization of his 'Graal' did not begin until after his death. It was the work of men who wished to erase every suspicion of heterodox or heretical elements. They continued his work and brought it to completion in a spirit totally alien to his and unrelated to his original intentions.

By interpreting the essence of his tale as a drama between heresy and faith, damnation and redemption, with the final victory assured for the latter, we may understand the poet's true purpose and so discover, both in his work and in that of his imitators, a reflection of some of the most dramatic occurrences in contemporary French civilization.

The Grail episodes in Chrétien's

'Conte del Graal'[1]

The Grail procession and the banquet of the Fisher King

3187 Et leanz avoit lumineire
      Si grant con l'an puet greignor feire
      De chandoiles an on ostel.

3190 Que qu'il parloient d'un et d'el,
      Uns vaslez d'une chanbre vint,
      Qui une blanche lance tint —
      Anpoigniee par le mileu,
      Si passa par antre le feu

3195 Et çaus qui el lit se seoient.
      Et tuit cil de leanz veoient
      La lance blanche et le fer blanc,
      S'issoit une gote de sanc
      Del fer de la lance an somet,

3200 Et jusqu'a la main au vaslet
      Coloit cele gote vermoille.
      Li vaslez vit cele mervoille
      Qui leanz ert la nuit venuz,
      Si c'est de demander tenuz

3205 Comant cele chose avenoit;
      Que del chasti li sovenoit
      Celui qui chevalier le fist,
      Qui li anseigna et aprist
      Que de trop parler se gardast,

[1] Alfons Hilka's edition.

3210   Si crient, se il le demandast,
       Qu'an il tenist a vilenie:
       Por ce si nel demanda mie.
       ATANT dui autre vaslet vindrent,
          Qui chandeliers an lor mains tindrent
3215   De fin or, ovrez a neel.
       Li vaslet estoient mout bel
       Qui les chandeliers aportoient;
       An chascun chandelier ardoient
       Dis chandoiles a tot le mains.
3220   Un graal antre ses deus mains
       Une dameisele tenoit,
       Qui avuec les vaslez venoit,
       Bele et jante et bien acesmee.
       Quant ele fu leanz antree
3225   Atot le graal qu'ele tint,
       Une si granz clartez i vint
       Qu'ausi perdirent les chandoiles
       Lor clarté come les estoiles
       Quant li solauz lieve ou la lune.
3230   Aprés celi an revint une
       Qui tint un tailleor d'arjant.
       Li graaus, qui aloit devant,
       De fin or esmeré estoit;
       Pierres precïeuses avoit
3235   El graal de maintes menieres,
       Des plus riches et des plus chieres
       Qui an mer ne an terre soient:
       Totes autres pierres passoient
       Celes del graal sanz dotance.
3240   Tot ausi con passa la lance

Par devant le lit s'an passerent
Et d'une chanbre an autre antrerent.
Et li vaslez les vit passer
Et n'osa mie demander
3245 Del graal cui l'an an servoit,
Que toz jorz an son cuer avoit
La parole au prodome sage,
Si criem que il n'i et domage
Por ce que j'ai oï retreire
3250 Qu'ausi bien se puet an trop teire
Con trop parler a la foiiee.
Ou bien l'an praingne ou mal l'an chiee,
Ne lor anquiert ne ne demande.
Et li sire au vaslet comande
3255 L'eve doner et napes treire.
Cil le font qui le doivent feire
Et qui acostumé l'avoient.
Li sire et li vaslez lavoient
Lor mains d'eve chaude tanpree.
3260 Et dui vaslet ont aportee
Une table lee d'ivoire:
Einsi con tesmoingne l'estoire,
Ele estoit tote d'une piece.
Devant le seignor une piece
3265 Et devant le vaslet la tindrent
Tant que dui autre vaslet vindrent,
Qui aporterent deus eschaces;
Le fuz an ot deus bones graces
Don les eschaces feites furent;
3270 Que les pieces toz jorz andurent.
Don furent eles? — D'ebenus. —

D'un fust a quoi? — Ja n'i bet nus
Que il porrisse ne qu'il arde;
De cez deus choses n'a il garde.

3275   Sor cez eschaces fu assise
La table, et la nape sus mise.
Mes que diroie de la nape?
Legaz ne chardonaus ne pape
Ne manja onques sor si blanche.

3280   Li premiers més fu d'une hanche
De cerf de greisse au poivre chaut.
Vins clers ne raspez ne lor faut
A cope d'or soëf a boivre.
De la hanche de cerf au poivre

3285   Uns vaslez devant aus trancha,
Qui a soi treite la hanche a
Atot le tailleor d'arjant,
Et les morsiaus lor met devant
Sor un gastel qui fu antiers.

3290   Et li graaus andemantiers
Par devant aus retrespassa,
Et li vaslez ne demanda
Del graal cui l'an an servoit:
Por le prodome se tenoit,

3295   Qui doucemant le chastia
De trop parler, et il i a
Toz jorz son cuer, si l'an sovient.
Mes plus se test qu'il ne covient,
Qu'a chascun més don l'an servoit

3300   Par devant lui trespasser voit
Le graal trestot descovert,
Mes il ne set cui l'an an sert,

Et si le voldroit mout savoir;
Mes il le demandera voir,
3305 Ce dit et panse, ainz qu'il s'an tort,
A un des vaslez de la cort,
Mes jusqu'au matin atandra
Que au seignor congié prandra
Et a tote l'autre meisniee.
3310 Einsi la chose a respitiee,
S'antant a boivre et a mangier;
L'an n'aporte mie a dangier
Les més ne le vin a la table,
Qui sont pleisant et delitable.
3315 LI mangiers fu et biaus et buens;
De toz les més que rois ne cuens
Ne anperere doie avoir
Fu li prodon serviz le soir,
Et li vaslez ansanble o lui.
3320 Aprés le mangier anbedui
Parlerent ansanble et veillierent.
Et li vaslet apareillierent
Les liz et le fruit au couchier;
Que il an i ot de mout chier:
3325 Dates, figues et noiz muscates
Et girofle et pomes grenates
Et leituaires an la fin
Et gingenbrat alixandrin
Et pliris aromaticon,
3330 Resontif et stomaticon.
Aprés si burent de maint boivre:
Pimant, ou n'ot ne miel ne poivre,
Et bon moré et cler sirop.

Perceval's confession and conversion

6372 Sire, chies le Roi Pescheor
   Fui une fois et vi la lance
   Don li fers sainne sanz dotance,
6375 Et de cele gote de sanc
   Que de la pointe del fer blanc
   Vi pandre, rien n'an demandai;
   Onques puis, certes, n'amandai.
   Et del graal que je i vi
6380 Ne soi pas cui l'an an servi,
   S'an ai puis eü si grant duel
   Que morz eüsse esté mon vuel,
   Et Damedeu an obliai,
   Qu'ainz puis merci ne li criai,
6385 Ne ne fis rien que je seüsse
   Par quoi ja mes merci eüsse."
   „HA! biaus amis," fet li prodon,
   „Or me di comant tu as non."
   Et il li dist: „Percevaus, sire."
6390 A cest mot li prodon sospire,
   Qui a le non reconeü,
   Et dit: „Frere, mout t'a neü
   Uns pechiez don tu ne sez mot:
   Ce fu li diaus que ta mere ot
6395 De toi quant tu partis de li;
   Que pasmee a terre cheï
   Au chief del pont devant la porte
   Et de cest duel fu ele morte.
   Por le pechié que tu an as
6400 T'avint que tu ne demandas

De la lance ne del graal,
Si t'an sont avenu maint mal,
Ne n'eüsses pas tant duré,
S'ele ne t'eüst comandé
6405 A Damedeu, ce saches tu.
Mes sa proiiere ot tel vertu
Que Deus por li t'a regardé
De mort et de prison gardé.
Pechiez la langue te trancha
6410 Quant le fer qui ainz n'estancha
De seignier devant toi veïs,
Ne la reison n'an anqueïs.
Et quant del graal ne seüs
Cui l'an an sert, fol san eüs:
6415 Cil cui l'an an sert, est mes frere;
Ma suer et soe fu ta mere,
Et del riche Pescheor croi
Que il est filz a celui roi
Qui del graal servir se fet.
6420 Mes ne cuidiez pas que il et
Luz ne lamproies ne saumon:
D'une sole oiste li sainz hon,
Que l'an an cest graal li porte,
Sa vie sostient et conforte;
6425 Tant sainte chose est li graaus,
Et il est si esperitaus
Qu'a sa vie plus ne covient
Que l'oiste qui el graal vient.
Quinze anz a ja esté einsi
6430 Que fors de la chanbre n'issi
Ou le graal veïs antrer.

Or te vuel anjoindre et doner
Penitance de ton pechié."
„Biaus oncles, einsi le vuel gié"
6435 Fet Percevaus, „mout de buen cuer.
Quant ma mere fu vostre suer,
Bien me devez neveu clamer
Et je vos oncle et miauz amer."
„Voirs est, biaus niés; mes ore antant:
6440 Se de t'ame pitiez te prant,
Si aies an toi repantance,
Et va el non de penitance
Au mostier einz qu'an autre leu
Chascun jor, si i avras preu,
6445 Et si ne leisse por nul plet,
Se tu es an leu ou il et
Mostier, chapele ne parroche,
Va la quant sonera la cloche
Ou, einçois, se tu es levez:
6450 Ja de ce ne seras grevez,
Einz an iert mout t'ame avanciee.
Et se la messe est comanciee,
Tant i fera il meillor estre,
Tant i demore que li prestre
6455 Avra tot dit et tot chanté.
Se ce te vient a volanté,
Ancor porras monter an pris,
S'avras enor et paradis.
Deu croi, Deu aimme, Deu aore,
6460 Buen home et buene fame enore,
Contre le provoire te lieve;
C'est uns servises qui po grieve,

Et Deus l'aimme por verité
Por ce qu'il vient d'umilité.

6465 Se pucele aïe te quiert,
Aïe li, que miauz t'an iert,
Ou veve dame ou orfeline;
Icele aumosne iert anterine:
Aïe lor, si feras bien.

6470 Garde ja nel leissier por rien:
Ce vuel que por tes pechiez faces,
Se ravoir viaus totes tes graces
Ausi con tu avoir les siaus.
Or me di se feire le viaus."

6475 „Oïl," fet il, „mout volantiers."
„Or te pri que deus jorz antiers
Avuec moi ceanz te remaingnes
Et que an penitance praingnes
Tel viande come est la moie."

6480 Et Percevaus le li otroie.
Et li hermites li consoille
Une oreison dedanz l'oroille,
Si li ferma tant qu'il la sot;
Et an cele oreison si ot

6485 Assez des nons nostre Seignor,
Car il i furent li greignor
Que nomer ne doit boche d'ome,
Se por peor de mort nes nome.
Quant l'oreison li ot aprise,

6490 Desfandi li qu'an nule guise
Ne la deïst sanz grant peril.
„Non ferai je, sire" fet il.
Einsi remest et si oï

E

Le servise et mout s'esjoï.
6495 Aprés le servise aora
La croiz et ses pechiez plora
Et se repanti duremant,
Et fu einsi tot coiemant.
Icele nuit a mangier ot
6500 Ice qu'au saint ermite plot;
Mes il n'i ot s'erbetes non,
Cerfuel, leitues et cresson
Et pain i ot d'orge et d'avainne
Et eve clere de fontainne;
6505 Et ses chevaus ot de l'estrain
Et de l'orge un bacin tot plain
Et estable tel come il dut:
Conreez fu si come estut.

EINSI Percevaus reconut
6510   Que Deus au vandredi reçut
Mort et si fu crocefiiez;
A la pasque comeniiez
Fu Percevaus mout dignemant.
De Perceval plus longuemant
6515 Ne parole li contes ci,
Einz avroiz mes assez oï
De mon seignor Gauvain parler
Que rien m'oiiez de lui conter.

Select Bibliography

PRINCIPAL EDITIONS

HILKA, A. *Der Percevalroman (Li Contes del Graal)* in *Christian von Troyes Sämtliche Werke*, herausgegeben von W. Förster, vol. v, Halle a S. (critical edition) 1932.

ROACH, WILLIAM. Chrétien de Troyes: *Le Roman de Perceval ou le Conte du Graal*, publié d'après le Ms. Fr. 12576 de la Bibliothèque Nationale, Genève-Lille, 1956 (2nd ed. 1959).

ROQUES, MARIO. The edition in the *Classiques Français du Moyen Age* had not appeared at the time of writing (1958–1960) but the Introduction had been published in *Romania*, LXXXI, pp. 1–36 (1960).

TRANSLATION INTO MODERN FRENCH

FOULET, L. *Le Conte du Graal*, Paris, 1947.

TRANSLATION INTO ENGLISH

LINKER, R. W. *The Story of the Grail*, University of North Carolina Press, Chapel Hill, N.C., 2nd ed. 1960.

RECENT STUDIES[1]

FOURRIER, A. In *Bulletin Bibliographique de la Société Internationale Arthurienne*, vol. VII, 1955, p. 89 f., sums up previous discussions of the date of the poem's composition and fixes the *terminus ad quem* at 1184. The precise date of composition has never been established, but 1180 would seem to be the mean.

---

[1] The bibliography of the *Conte del Graal* is too vast to be included here. A few of the recent titles should suffice.

FRAPPIER, JEAN. *Chrétien de Troyes*, Paris, 1957, pp. 170–209.
HOFER, STEFAN. *Chrétien de Troyes: Leben und Werke des altfranzösischen Epikers*, Graz-Köln, 1954, ch. XIII.

LEJEUNE, RITA. In *Bulletin Bibliographique, etc.*, vol. IX, 1957, p. 85 f., proposes the date of 1178–80. The debate continued in the *Bulletin*, X, 1958, p. 73 f.
LOOMIS, ROGER SHERMAN. *Arthurian Literature in the Middle Ages (a collaborative history)*, Oxford University Press, 1959. This may be used as a bibliographical guide to the various subjects and problems and for the *Conte del Graal* within the general setting of the Arthurian traditions.

REVIEWS AND STUDIES OF
'IL CASTELLO DEL RE PESCATORE'

Cahiers de Civilisation Médiévale, IV, no. 4, Octobre–Décembre 1961, pp. 475–80 (Pierre Gallais, 'Perceval et la conversion de sa famille: A propos d'un article récent'). Reviewed by V. Bertolucci, *Studi francesi*, 17, 1962, p. 321.
Studi Francesi, 16, 1962, pp. 120–1 (R. de Cesare).
Lettres Romanes, 16, 1962, pp. 81–2 (A. G.).
Romania, LXXXV, 1964, pp. 381–9 (Félix Lecoy).

Notes

a Even this sequel does not reveal all the castle's secrets. It does, however, end Perceval's search for the Grail, which is followed by an account of Gawain's amorous and chivalric adventures. The break in the story is clearly marked in l. 6514 f.:

> De Perceval plus longuemant
> Ne parole li contes ci,
> Einz avroiz mes assez oï
> De mon seignor Gauvain parler
> Que rien m'oiiez de lui conter.

The poem goes on to recount the chivalrous adventures of Gawain without further mention of Perceval or the Grail, in a spirit that is quite different from that of the rest of the tale. This would seem to justify E. Hoepffner's theory (already to be found in Gustav Gröber's *Grundriss der Romanischen Philologie*, Strassburg, 1902, vol. II, part 1, p. 504 f.), according to which this long epilogue is nothing but an unfinished account of Gawain's adventures arbitrarily added by one of Chrétien's earliest *remanieurs* (cf. *Romania*, LX, 1939, p. 412 f.). More recently Martin de Riquer in his 'Perceval y Gauvain en *Li Contes del Graal*' (*Filologia Romanza*, IV, 1957, pp. 119–47), has restated the hypothesis of two independent romances left unfinished at Chrétien's death—the one dedicated to Perceval, the other to Gawain's adventures—which were arbitrarily amalgamated by an early redactor in ll. 4688–746. Jean Frappier has resolutely rejected this hypothesis ('Sur la composition du Conte du Graal', *Moyen Age*, LXIV, 1958, p. 67 f.).

Admittedly, Chrétien's poem, composed of various discon-
nected and seemingly independent episodes, shows a tendency
to lose the thread of the plot and to interrupt it by new episodes, but this is already the case in one of Chrétien's earlier
poems, *Del Chevalier de la Charrete*, which inaugurates the
adventures of Lancelot du Lac. Such an arrangement is typical
of all later chivalric poetry and prose, including Ariosto's
Orlando Furioso (cf. my *La poesia italiana del Cinquecento*,
Firenze, 1933, p. 14). The great expert on medieval French
epic, Philip Emanuel Becker, considered Chrétien's poem spu-
rious from l. 3427 onward, i.e. interrupted at that point and
then terminated by some unknown authors. The break, according to Becker, occurred as early as the episode of Perceval's departure from the Fisher King's Castle—almost at the
beginning of his adventures (cf. 'Von den Erzählern neben
und nach Chrestien de Troyes', *Zeitschrift für Romanische Philologie*, LV, 1935, p. 400 f.). All these views appear to find some
justification in the seemingly incoherent structure of the poem,
which is rich in ambiguities, contradictions, and unfinished
episodes. But the answer is to be found, at least so far as the
first part of the poem is concerned, in the narrative technique
of any such *ambages pulcherrimae* and in the inner structure of
Chrétien's poem: Perceval's conversion (ll. 6217–513) is its
fulfilment and not, as De Riquer would have it, a later inter-
polation. Cf. J. Frappier, *Romania*, LXXXI, 1960, p. 308 f.

b This great personage, regent of the kingdom of France
before the death of Louis VII in 1179–80, *vir magne sapientie
et potentie*, as he is described by a contemporary chronicler
(cf. A. Cartellieri, *Philipp II August, König von Frankreich*,
Leipzig–Paris, 1899–1900, vol. I, Appendix, p. 16), maintained
close political and family ties with the court of Champagne at
Troyes, especially after 1168, when he took over control of
Flanders. He then proceeded to take more effective and more
violent measures of repression against this centre of heretical

expansion than the king of France had hitherto dared to employ (cf. C. Schmidt, *Histoire et Doctrine de la secte des Cathares ou Albigeois*, vol. I, Paris–Genève, 1849, pp. 86–94). Chrétien, who was in his service from 1180 onwards (cf. S. Hofer, op. cit., p. 200, and A. Fourrier, op. cit., p. 89 f.), said of Philip in the prologue to the *Conte del Graal* (ll. 25–6) that he loved 'droite justise/Et leauté et sainte iglise', and extolled him as a ruler superior to Alexander the Great, then praised Philip's charity, largesse, and nobility.

page 2

a This distinction between the *matière*, or subject, of his poems and their *sen*, or significance, is set forth in the prologue to *Lancelot*. The *matière*, however, does not concern us here. It has been widely studied, although critics have been unable to reach agreement as to its provenance. One group of scholars looks for its origins in ancient Celtic traditions, but such evidence as there is belongs to a later period and is therefore hardly decisive (cf. Roger Sherman Loomis, *Arthurian Tradition and Chrétien de Troyes*, New York, Columbia University Press, 1949; Jean Marx, *La légende arthurienne et le Graal*, Paris, 1952; and W. A. Nitze, *Perceval and the Holy Grail: an Essay on the Romance of Chrétien de Troyes*, Berkeley–Los Angeles, University of California Publications in Modern Philology, XXVIII, 5, 1949, who adds further doubtful Romance and Byzantine elements to the supposedly Celtic sources). A certain success was enjoyed for a time by Jessie L. Weston's book, *From Ritual to Romance* (Cambridge, 1920), —an attempt to link the Grail story with ancient pagan rites and symbols (agrarian, phallic, and so on) which secretly survived the coming of Christianity; yet since it is impossible to see how these can have inspired a Christian poet in the second half of the twelfth century, the more realistic students of Chrétien's work take little notice of this theory. The view

that the Grail is a myth of Islamic origins has recently been
revived by Pierre Ponsoye in *L'Islam et le Graal* (Paris, 1957),
while Biblical and Judaic sources have been used in similar
fashion by Urban T. Holmes, Jr., and Sister M. Amelia
Klenke, O.P. (*Chrétien, Troyes and the Grail,* University of
North Carolina Press, 1959), who have gone as far as to transform the poet into a convert from Judaism to Christianity
and then into a kind of poetic missionary, writing in the spirit
of Walter of Châtillon's *Tractatus contra Judaeos*—a thesis which
has failed to gain acceptance because it sets out to prove too
much. The words spoken by one of Chrétien's characters, 'li
faus juïf... c'on devroit tüer come chiens' (6292–3) would
seem to rule out any intention to 'convert by poetry'. Their
vehemence is in accord with contemporary habits of thought
and speech, with the religious policy of Philip of Flanders,
aimed at the extermination of all Jews and heretics, and no
doubt with the poet's own feelings. There happens to be
exactly the same type of outburst in the *Haut Livre du Graal*
(*Perlesvaus*), which belongs to the first years of the thirteenth
century (ed. Nitze and Jenkins, 2 vols, Chicago University
Press, 1932–4), as R. S. Loomis has noted in *Romania,* LXXXI,
1960, p. 498. The same expressions are used against converts as
can be seen in Ch. V. Langlois, *La Vie en France au Moyen Age,*
vol. II, Paris, 1925, p. 66, n. 1. Nor does anything either in
the *Conte del Graal* or in the later versions of the story justify
the new thesis put forward by Helen Adolf in *Visio Pacis—
Holy City and Grail* (Pennsylvania State University, 1960)
with a view to showing that the Grail in Chrétien represents
the Holy Sepulchre and the City of Jerusalem, which the
Christian world lost in 1187. Konrad Burdach's writings on
the Byzantine origins of the legend (especially his large
volume *Der Graal,* Stuttgart, 1939) have enjoyed a certain
amount of notoriety, but contributed little to a positive interpretation of Chrétien's poem. For supposedly Persian sources

see Lars-Jvar Ringbom's somewhat confused argument in *Graltempel und Paradies*, Stockholm, 1951 (*Kungl. Vitterhets Historie och Antikvitets Akademiens Handlingar Del* 73), a work which deals mainly with the continuators of Wolfram von Eschenbach, and A. U. Pope, 'Persia and the Holy Grail', *Literary Review*, 1, 1957, p. 57 f. Neither of these two works has much bearing on Chrétien's *Conte del Graal*.

The fanaticism displayed by all these critics and their followers leads them to explore *ignotum per ignotius*, to invent fantastic etymologies for the names found in the Arthurian tradition, to seize upon any clue offered by doubtful or authenticated sources and to embroider the few facts that we are able to deduce from the latter. Moreover, no one has been able to explain in a satisfactory manner how these Celtic, Oriental, popular, and esoteric traditions can have been handed down to Chrétien de Troyes or his source or why they fascinated his public and the men of letters of the late Middle Ages. For the most recent interpretations of the poem's mysteries see 'Les Romans du Graal dans la littérature des XIIe et XIIIe siècles', *Colloques internationaux du Centre National de la Recherche Scientifique*, Paris, 1956 (henceforward, *Colloques, etc.*) as well as the miscellany edited by René Nelli, *Lumière du Graal*, Paris, 1951. To avoid such confusion and the sectarianism of the various schools, we must keep within the bounds of good sense and poetic necessity determined by the chronological and spiritual limits of Chrétien's age. Süheila Bayrad's opinion, expressed in *Symbolisme médiéval* (Paris–Istanbul, 1957, p. 82), that it is impossible 'd'apprécier à sa juste valeur l'art et les intentions de l'écrivain tant qu'on ne peut distinguer son apport personnel de la matière que lui fournissait la tradition' is surely open to question. If this were the case the critics would have to for go the attempt to arrive at a direct interpretation of any poem whose sources are not known.

page 3

a When Perceval asks what an 'iglise' and 'mostier' are, his mother replies (ll. 577–82):

> . . . Filz, ce meïsme:
> Une meison bele et saintisme
> Et de cors sainz et de tresors,
> S'i sacrefie l'an le cors
> Jesucrist la prophete sainte
> Cui giu firent honte mainte.

The expression 'S'i sacrefie l'an le cors Jesucrist' is interesting because the idea of the Mass as a sacrifice was at that time a subject for theological discussion, opposed to the fairly common interpretation of the service as *memoria passionis* (cf. J. A. Jungmann, S.J., *Missarum Solemnia*, Vienna, 1948, I, p. 224 f.), variously accepted and broadcast by heterodox and heretical sects (cf. A. Borst, *Die Katharer*, Schriften der *Monumenta Germaniae Historica*, vol. XII, Stuttgart, 1953). With regard to Perceval's faulty religious education, cf. the debate between O. Jodogne, 'Le sens chrétien de jeune Perceval dans "Le Conte du Graal" ', *Lettres Romanes*, XIV, 1960, pp. 111–21, and Mario Roques, *Romania*, LXXXI, 1960, p. 271 f.

b The expression 'cel seignor' may be taken as a simple translation of 'ille dominus'. However, 'la prophete sainte' brings to mind not only the Moslems (who accept Jesus as a mere prophet), but also the beliefs of the Manichaeans and their disciples in Chrétien's France. They recognized in Christ the Saviour announced by the Old Testament (which they rejected as inspired by the devil), and especially—like Mani himself and Mohammed later—the apostle of salvation (cf. Henri-Charles Puech's *Le Manichéisme*, Paris, Musée Guimet, Bibliothèque de Diffusion, tome LVI, 1949, ch. II; and on the heretical sects in the Middle Ages, A. Borst, op. cit., p. 162 f.).

The concept of Christ the prophet clearly belongs to Gnostic tradition and is extraneous to orthodox Christianity. Hence the difficulty of explaining its presence at the beginning of the *Conte del Graal* except as an indication of the author's awareness of the religious and theological doubts that troubled contemporary Christendom.

c Chrétien's religious phraseology is for the most part scant and quite conventional, as has been pointed out by W. Kellermann in 'Aufbaustil and Weltbild Chrestiens von Troyes', *Beihefte zur Zeitschrift für romanische Philologie*, LXXXVIII, p. 87 f., Halle (Saale) 1936, and by P. Imbs in 'L'élément religieux dans *le Conte del Graal* de Chrétien de Troyes', *Colloques*, *etc.*, III, p. 36 f.

page 4

a For this development cf. Emile Mâle, *L'art religieux du xiiie siècle en France*, 6th ed., Paris, 1953, and K. Künstle, *Ikonographie der christlichen Kunst*, 2 vols, Freiburg i. B., 1928, esp. I, p. 239 f., with bibliography. Except for traditional representations of the Last Judgment, angels and demons first appear in French art in the twelfth century, with a prevalence of gruesome, individual devils.

b On the lively angelological (and demonological) controversy in the twelfth century, when angelic images were added to the archangels and to the celestial hierarchies of biblical and patristic tradition, see the articles *Anges* and *Démons* in the *Dictionnaire de Théologie Catholique* by Vacant and Mangenot, vol. I, 1935, col. 1222 f., and IV, 1924, part I, col. 384 f. For more recent studies of biblical, evangelical and liturgical precedents see the essays by Burkhard Neunheuser, O.S.B., Heinrich Gross and Heinrich Schlier in *Archiv für Liturgiewissenschaft*, vol. VI, 1959, pp. 4–61. For heretical teachings on the subject, which are fundamental for an understanding of contemporary theology, cf. A. Borst, op. cit., esp.

pp. 144–56, 162 f. and passim, while the reader may profit-
ably consult one of the few authentic documents of the
Catharist heresy, such as the *Liber de Duobus Principiis* edited
with an excellent introduction by A. Dondaine, O.P., Istituto
Storico Domenicano di Santa Sabina, Rome, 1939. Although
of Italian origin and composed about the middle of the thirteenth century, this text preserves certain traditional elements
that go back to the eleventh and twelfth centuries and, more
or less directly, to Bogomil, Byzantine, Gnostic, and Manichaean sources of obscure yet certain origin. On the doubts
expressed by various critics see R. Morghen, 'L'eresia nel
Medio Evo', *Medioevo Cristiano* (Bari, 1951, esp. p. 271 f.).
Manichaean traditions must have been kept alive during the
heterodox renewal of religious thought in that age by the intense anti-Manichaean controversy in St Augustine, who was
the most frequently read and discussed of the Fathers of the
Church. In the Catharist tract quoted above we find the statement (p. 109) that God cannot have created 'angelos demones
neque tenebrosos, sed claros angelos et luminosos'. The controversy left its mark in Wolfram von Eschenbach's *Parzifal*.
Here, in two famous passages (Lib. IX, 454, l. 21 f. and Lib.
XVI, 798, l. 2 f., respectively pp. 219 and 375 of K. Lachmann's
critical edition, 7th ed., Berlin, 1952, and vol. II of the ed.
with a commentary by K. Bartsch and M. Marti, Leipzig,
1932), the author, while discussing the salvation of the so-
called neutral angels, expresses opinions that are frankly defined as heretical by Bartsch and Marti (ed. cit., I, p. xxxviii)
and are a frequent subject for debate (cf. P. Wapnewski,
Wolframs Parzifal, *etc.*, Heidelberg, 1955, p. 154 f., and H. J.
Koppitz, *Wolframs Religiosität*, *etc.*, dissertation, Bonn, 1958,
p. 326). On these concepts, which are quite foreign to Thomistic angelology and akin to Dante's, see Bruno Nardi's important studies, 'Gli angeli che non furon ribelli né fur fedeli
a Dio' in *Lectura Dantis Siciliana*, Alcamo, Accademia di Studi

'Cielo d'Alcamo', 1959, and *L'Alighieri*, Rassegna Biblio-
grafica Dantesca, I, 1960, p. 59.

c The basic difference between the orthodox and the heretical interpretation of these two cosmic concepts lies in the
fact that the former considers light and darkness as attributes
of God and Satan respectively, while for the latter they have
their essence in the characteristic dualism of a god of light,
creator of the spiritual world, and a god of darkness, creator
of the sensible world; that is to say, of good and evil respectively, each of which is independent and autonomous in its
workings. Cf. the works quoted in note 4*a* above, as well as
C. Schmidt's classic work (op. cit., esp. II, p. 12 f.) and
F. Tocco's *L'Eresia nel Medio Evo* (Firenze, 1884, esp. Lib. I).
For the orthodox concept of the Augustinian *Splendor, Fulgor,
Species, Claritas*, according to St Bernard and medieval theology, and for its influence on contemporary aesthetics and
artistic creation, cf. C. Bäumker's *Witelo, ein Philosoph und
Naturforscher des XIII Jahrhunderts*, Münster, 1908 ('Beiträge
zur Geschichte und Philosophie des Mittelalters', Bd. III,
Heft 2) and my article on 'Sacra Doctrina e Theologia Mys-
tica', *Giornale Dantesco*, vol. XXXVI, N.S., VI (Annuario Dantesco)
1933–4. Joseph A. Mazzeo's *Structure and Thought in the Para-
diso* (Ithaca, N.Y., Cornell University Press, 1958, pp. 68–83
and passim) contains further material on the subject, as does
Otto von Simson's *Gothic Cathedral* (Bollingen Series, New
York, 1956, vol. XLVIII, pp. 50 f., 119 f., and passim). For
ancient and early Christian examples the reader may consult
the forthcoming article *Φῶς* in the monumental *Theologisches Wörterbuch zum Neuen Testament* by G. Kittel and
G. Friedrich. St John's Gospel is the only place in Scripture
where God is identified with light in a literal sense. For the
Bible tells us that God creates, but is not, light. According to
the Neoplatonic-Christian tradition, light emanates from God.
Philo Judaeus (d. Alexandria, 50 A.D.) is the first to regard

God (*de Somniis*, I, 75) as the primordial archetype of light, thus creating the concept of the God of Light which was taken up by the Evangelist and especially discussed by St Irenaeus (*Adversus Haereses*, Lib. II, 4, 23).

page 5

a This point is indisputable, although towards the end of his *Parzifal* Wolfram states that he draws his inspiration from a poem by 'Kyōt der Provenzāl' (Lib. XVI, 827 f.) who has been tentatively identified as the French poet Guiot de Provins, supposedly the author of another poem about Perceval, which is completely unknown and which has been the object of numberless contradictory speculations. Cf. note 44*a*.

b III, 119, 17, cf. Lachmann's ed. cit., p. 66 and vol. I, p. 142 of Bartsch and Marti's ed. cit. The same question is repeated and accompanied by violent expressions of hatred of God by Perceval, as a full-grown man (IV, 332, I). In Wolfram's work he appears as a rebel, while in Chrétien's poem he is merely ignorant of certain divine mysteries which he does not attempt to understand: he sins through ignorance and not through malice, according to the distinction made by contemporary theologians and moralists, based on St Augustine (cf. the *Dictionnaire de Théologie Catholique*, vol. XII, part I, col. 194 f., and the article 'Ignorance' in the same work). In the *Conte del Graal* the question is not explicit, but the hero's attitude reflects a state of mind typical of his age. The problem of the nature, essence, and attributes of God had forced itself not only upon the great pre-scholastics such as St Anselm, Peter Lombard, Gilbert de la Porée, and many other theologians (as well as the contemporary clergy and the faithful), but also upon heterodox thinkers, doubtful believers, and the numerous heretical proselytizers. This led to a renewal and consolidation of the faith by means of synods, councils, inquisitors, and—finally—the Thomistic system, designed to be the definitive

Catholic answer. Cf. M. Chossat's exhaustive article in the *Dictionnaire de Théologie Catholique* already quoted, vol. IV, col. 1152 f., and, for the heretics, *A. Borst*, op. cit., pp. 151-6. The period of most intense activity and discussion of these tendencies in both camps extends from 1140 to 1180, and corresponds to the years of Chrétien's maturity and Wolfram's youth.

> c   Son, I tell you truly:
> He is far more bright than the light of day . . .
> His mother clearly separated for him
> Resplendent light from darkness.
>
> (Lib. III, 119, 18 f.)

These are not metaphors, but the precise terms of a metaphysical antithesis doctrinally elaborated by heretical sects of the twelfth century, as recent scholars have pointed out in their studies of such influences in Wolfram's poem. Among these studies we would single out, in spite of some exaggerated remarks, Edwin H. Zeydel, 'Wolframs Parzifal, Kyot und die Katharer', *Neophilologus*, XXXVII, 1953, pp. 25-35, and, for this particular case, esp. p. 32, where the author quite rightly emphasizes the fact that in this passage the god of light is explicitly opposed to Satan 'der helle wirt, der ist swarz' (loc. cit., ll. 25-6), while Parzifal is warned never to think of him and not to give way to doubt. Judgments to the contrary, but hardly convincing, are made in P. B. Wessels' 'Wolfram zwischen Dogma und Legende', *Beiträge zur Geschichte der deutschen Sprache und Literatur*, vol. 77, 1955, pp. 112-35, and more moderately and perceptively in P. Wapnewski, op. cit., pp. 66 f. and 174 f., who nevertheless acknowledges certain vague Gnostic and Manichaean tendencies in the Grail saga. Why not extend this to Chrétien's *Conte del Graal*? Is it possible to believe that poets of such rank, living in the most important centres of intellectual and political activity in their countries, were left unmoved by the great spiritual tendencies of their times? Such influences as are to be found in their works do not imply adherence to any particular sect or doctrine, but merely illustrate the way in which the various sects and doctrines were reflected in the author's imagination and feelings. The idea that Wolfram may have undergone Gnostic and Manichaean influences through the Catharist teachings of the times is to be found in other studies quoted by Zeydel and Wapnewski. Yet these were always accompanied by hypothetical references to 'Kyōt der Provenzāl', about whom nothing certain has yet been discovered, perhaps, as Otto Rahn suggests in *Kreuzzug gegen den Graal* (Freiburg i. Breisgau, 1933), because the romance he is supposed to have written with Perceval as its hero (explicitly mentioned by Wolfram) was destroyed by the inquisitors on account of its supposedly heretical character. It is, however, far more probable that the various scattered references to Catharist or heterodox doctrines in Wolfram's poem (already adumbrated in Chrétien's *Conte del Graal*) belong to a religious phraseology and theological concepts that were widespread in the troubled spiritual climate of the twelfth century. For a detailed history of the metaphysical contrast between light and darkness in various religions see the index in J. Hasting's *Encyclopaedia of Religion and Ethics*, vol. VIII, 1921, pp. 47–66. For the Hebraic-Christian tradition, expressed esp. in St John's Gospel (ch. 1) and in his first epistle, cf. ibid. p. 22 f. It should, however, be remembered that the strictly monotheistic character of this tradition sets it quite apart from the Gnostic dualism of Persian origin perpetuated in Manichaeism and related sects.

page 6

a Cf. A. Dondaine, *Liber de Duobus Principiis, etc.*, Rome, 1939, p. 83; A. Borst, *Die Katharer*, Stuttgart, 1953, pp. 144 f., 149 f., and passim. A brief but excellent account of this doctrine is to be found in F. Tocco's *L'eresia nel Medio Evo* (Firenze, 1884, p. 73 f.). For a history of the concept of the 'creatio ex nihilo', as opposed to the 'creatio ex essentia Dei', cf. H. A. Wolfson in *Medieval Studies in Honor of J. D. M. Ford*, Harvard University Press, Cambridge, Mass., 1948, p. 355 f.

b This first, chief sin committed by the young hero (cf. l. 6392 f.) and those of which he is at times accused—and for which he finally does penance—are not in fact caused by diabolical intervention, his own will, or by any other motive discussed in medieval theology (cf. the exhaustive treatment of these concepts until the thirteenth century in the *Dictionnaire de Théol. Cath.*, XII, col. 140–462), but by a fatal inclination that accompanies his ignorance and persistent religious indifference. The denial of man's free will is one of the basic principles of Catharist teaching, reflecting as it does remote Oriental origins of the doctrine. Cf. Dondaine, op. cit., esp. p. 90 f.; Borst, op. cit., esp. p. 174 f.; C. Schmidt, *Histoire et Doctrine de la Secte des Cathares ou Albigeois*, Paris, 1849, vol. II, p. 79 f.; Tocco, op. cit., Lib. I, ch. I.

page 7

a The very opening of Wolfram's poem expresses the fundamental idea:

> Ist zwīvel herzen nāchgebūr
> Das muoz der sēle werden sūr, . . .

The poet thus warns the reader of the great threat to man's soul represented by doubt which is understood here as spiritual uncertainty. The word is used in this sense on several occasions throughout the poem (ed. cit., 119, 28; 311, 22; 371, 4; etc.) and has been the subject of much discussion, some of it excessively subtle. Cf. P. Wapnewski's excellent analysis in *Wolframs 'Parzifal'*, Heidelberg, 1955, p. 15 f. and passim.

F

b For this evident, yet much debated, phenomenon see A. Borst, op. cit., p. 107 n. 37. The well known violent anti-papal invectives of Walter von der Vogelweide, one of Wolfram's contemporaries, which were akin to the sentiments of the heretics at the time of the Albigensian crusade, are typical. For the situation in France, cf. Raymond Foreville and Jean Rousset de Pina, in *Histoire de l'Eglise* fondée par A. Fliche et V. Martin, vol. IX, Paris, 1953, esp. ch. III and IV, as well as A. Fliche, ibid., vol. X, ch. IV (with extensive bibliography).

page 9

a See my 'La Cattedrale di Modena e il suo rilievo arturiano', *Archivum Romanicum*, vol. XIX, no. 2, 1935, courteously criticized by R. S. Loomis in *Studi Medievali*, N.S., 1936, pp. 1–17. The latter (cf. *Arthurian Literature in the Middle Ages*, Oxford, 1959, p. 60) continues to assert that the famous decorated archivolt in Modena cathedral dates from the years 1099–1120, 'according to Italian, German, and English art historians'. Emile Mâle, *L'Art Religieux du XIIe siècle en France*, 6th ed., Paris, 1953, p. 370, justly attributed it to the latter part of the twelfth century, while in a letter to me he stated: 'j'ai vu avec grand plaisir que vous considériez la sculpture de ce portail comme postérieure à 1150—et sur ce point je suis tout à fait d'accord avec vous'. According to the arguments put forward in my article, the famous bas-relief is, like other representations of knights and warriors in medieval cathedrals, an emblem of the *ordo militum*. With its portrayal of scenes from the life of the local saint, San Giminiano, added on to the Arthurian episode, it symbolizes the three classes that contributed to the building of this church: those who serve God by arms, by church worship, and by manual work, according to the social order which was thought to have been instituted by God. Seen in this light the bas-relief is certainly not a proof of the popularity of the Arthurian legend among the local populace or among the pilgrims who followed the *via francigena*.

b Another reading, according to A. Hilka's ed. (l. 3083), would be *sale pavée* instead of *quarreé*, (see Select Bibliography). These are purely conventional details found over and over again in various descriptions of both real and imaginary palaces in the contemporary *chansons de geste*. Cf. my *Paris nach den altfranzösischen nationalen Epen*, Heidelberg, 1913, pp. 29 f., 82 f., and 99 f.

c The description of this setting is exceedingly sober and functional, with no mention of those decorative elements that are so common, and at times catalogued with a multitude of details, in the *chansons de geste*. This excludes the possibility that this scene may represent, as Urban T. Holmes and Sister M. A. Klenke suggest, op. cit., p. 80, some kind of religious service or holy place, like Solomon's temple; or that the Castle of the Grail may signify the kingdom of the dead and the other life, as we find in A. Pauphilet, *Le Legs du Moyen Age*, Melun, 1950, p. 173 f. It was Wolfram von Eschenbach who later embroidered these simple data (see *Parzifal*, v, 229, 23 f. etc.) and thus encouraged his commentators to indulge in learned speculations without taking into account the fact that such descriptions of imaginary palaces with exotic elements are to be found in French and Provençal epics of the twelfth and thirteenth centuries, of which *Girard de Roussillon* is an outstanding example.

page 11

a The two protagonists are the only ones that actually partake of the banquet, while Wolfram von Eschenbach's far more elaborate description makes all the knights participate (*Parzifal*, v, 237 f.). The ivory table rests on two movable trestles of ebony, as was the custom—sometimes with other materials—at banquets at medieval and Renaissance courts. Cf. *Doon de Nanteuil* (P. Meyer, *Romania*, 1884, p. 1 f.): 'Charles vint a Paris. . . . Et font mettre les tables sur maint tretel d'ivoire' (ll. 120–1), and Baldassar Castiglione's 'Lettera al Cardinal Bibbiena del 2 novembre 1520' in *Lettere di Principi*, Venezia, 1570, vol. I, p. 71. This detail was in fact mentioned earlier in the famous *Letter of Prester John* of 1165, in which 'columpnae quae sustinent mensas ex ebore' constitute one of the elements of the imaginary palace that inspired so many fanciful descriptions of buildings in medieval romances. For this text see the critical edition by F. Zarncke, 'Der Priester Johannes', in *Abhandlung der Kgl. Sächsischen Gesellschaft der Wissenschaften*, Philol.-Hist. Classe, vol. VII, 1879, p. 918, 59. All this suggests than the banquet scene in the *Conte del Graal* is purely courtly and chivalric in character and that it is useless to look for hidden allusions to exotic mysteries in the references to ivory and ebony.

page 13

a This is also questioned among others by Stefan Hofer (p. 41); (see his work listed in the Bibliography). It is interesting to reflect on the type of canon Chrétien de Troyes would have made, since in the prologue to his *Conte del Graal* (l. 49) he attributes the expression *Deus caritas est*, etc., to St Paul instead of St John (I John, 4: 16; cf. A. Hilka, ed. cit., p. 617). Such an elementary mistake merely goes to show that it is impossible to endow Chrétien—who had until then remained faithful to his vocation as a worldly poet—with all the theological subtleties that Mme M. Lot-Borodine ('Le Conte del Graal de Chrétien de Troyes et sa présentation symbolique', *Romania*, LXXVII, 1956, pp. 235–88) discovers in the episode. To insist as she does on its liturgical character and on the interpretation of the Grail as a 'vase de la Grâce eucharistique' is to ignore the sacrilegious incongruities of the scene.

b Robert de Boron, *Le Roman de l'Estoire dou Graal*, edited by W. A. Nitze in the *Classiques français du Moyen Age*, 1927, ll. 935 f. and passim. The relationship between the two poems has been established by E. Hoepffner in his article in *Colloques*, etc.

c Wauchier de Denain, who wrote a sequel to the *Conte* about the year 1200, was the first to identify this lance with the spear that pierced Christ's side, according to St John (John 19: 34). Robert de Boron does not mention it, while in Chrétien's poem and those of his immediate continuators the lance plays a role that is completely independent of the Grail.

page 14

a In the twelfth century, according to Gérard de Cambrai, it was possible for a woman to bear in her hands *sacrum corpus Domini* to the sick (see A. Hilka's note, ed. cit., to l. 3221, p. 682). Mario Roques ('Le Graal de Chrétien et la Demoiselle au Graal', *Romania*, LXXVI, 1955, pp. 1–27, also Genève–Lille, 1955), basing himself on the religious iconography of the period, considers the 'Demoiselle du Graal' to be an allegory of the Church, and the Grail itself the chalice of the Last Supper or the ciborium used in the Mass. However, the comparison with the medieval images examined by Roques does not hold good, because such representations always appear in some sacred setting or context and are consequently easily identifiable; whereas the castle of the Grail and the hall in which the Grail appears are devoid of the most indispensable attributes and indications of Christian worship. An ecclesiastical or canonical interpretation of the characters and objects in the scene is therefore automatically ruled out. As Jean Marx aptly remarked in *Moyen Age*, LXIII, 1957, p. 469 f., none of Chrétien's imitators ever took up this interpretation, although it would clearly have strengthened the story's apologetical value. It is therefore impossible to see in this 'grailophorous damsel', who is 'bele et gente et bien acesmee' (l. 3223), an allegory of the Church. Such a view would be not only incomprehensible, but repugnant to a good Catholic.

b Cf. the discussion between A. Micha, *Romania*, LXXII, 1951, p. 238 f., and Jean Frappier, ibid., LXXIII, 1952, n. 6, p. 82 f., and LXXIV, 1953, p. 358. The latter refuses to regard the Grail as a Christian relic. See, moreover, his note in the *Bulletin de la Société Internationale Arthurienne*, VI, 1954, p. 75 f. On the form of these supposedly Eucharistic objects see the exhaustive work by Joseph Braun, S.J., *Das Christliche Altargerät in seinem Sein und in seiner Entwicklung*, München, 1932. This profusely illustrated, fundamental work seems to have been overlooked by the various scholars who have made so many surmises about the ciberia, patens, chalices, and other sacred objects supposed to be connected with the Grail, instead of referring to Joseph Braun's minute description of their history, shape, materials, significance, and usage.

page 15

a This fact has been rightly emphasized by R. S. Loomis in his works already quoted and in others, which have been systematically attacked by S. Hofer, op. cit., pp. 184–219, and which continue to be ignored by many scholars who cling to a Christian interpretation of the episode. For Loomis, however, its profane or pagan character serves to strengthen the view that its symbols are based on Celtic prototypes—a hypothesis more recently put forward by W. A. Nitze, op. cit., and Jean Marx, *La légende arthurienne et le Graal*, Paris, 1952 (Bibliothèque de l'Ecole des Hautes Etudes, Sciences Religieuses, LXVI). Jean Frappier in *Romania*, LXXIII, 1952, p. 92, and LXXIV, p. 367, as well as in his book quoted in the Bibliography, denies any direct connection between Chrétien's text and the rites of the Church.

b This definition is to be found in Migne, *Patr. lat.*, CCXIII,

814-15. Various etymologies have been proposed, but the object's shape and function have never been ascertained (see C. T. Gossen, 'Zur etymologischen Deutung des Grals', *Vox Romanica*, XVIII, 1959, no. 2, p. 180 n.). Mario Roques, in *Colloques, etc.* ('Le nom du Graal', pp. 5-13), has resolved the problem and proved that both the Latin term and its French and Provençal derivatives were commonly used to signify 'des récipients à ouverture large, plutôt profunds et hauts de bords', even as they are described by the chronicler, who is only slightly younger than Chrétien.

Wolfram's Grail is not a receptacle at all, but a stone of great luminosity which he calls *lapsit exillīs* (Lib. IX, 469, 7) and which has been variously interpreted. The only thing that it has in common with Chrétien's Grail is the intense brilliance that comes from the supernatural light given forth by both objects, a detail that shows clearly enough that it is not its form, but the light itself, that determines its essence and function.

c ll. 6417-31. Perceval's own statement (ll. 6379-80): 'Et del Graal que je i vi/Ne soi pas cui l'an an servi' clearly proves that it has no direct association with the Fisher King, his court, or his guest. Chrétien's imitators, however, conferred upon it the power of feeding the guests with fine dishes—'ce qui est une merveille sans noblesse et un contre-sens certain sur la pensée de Chrétien', as Mario Roques rightly observes in his preface to the translation of the *Conte del Graal* into Modern French by L. Foulet, Paris, 1947, p. xxiii.

page 16

a Cf. Mme Lot-Borodine in *Romania*, LXXVII, 1956, p. 235 f., who nevertheless persists in asserting the Christian and liturgical character of this episode. She is followed by C. Guerrieri-Crocetti in *Filologia Romanza*, VI, 1959, p. 130 f.

page 18

a This king father has received scant attention from critics. He disappears completely from the poems of Wolfram and of Chrétien's continuators, in which all the drama is concentrated on the figure of the invalid, Wolfram's Anfortas, whose name has been associated with the Latin *infirmitas* and French *enferté*. For this controversial etymology, see the commentaries and articles quoted *supra*. It is interesting to note that the enigmatic, and therefore suspicious, figure of the penitent who lives on the host contained in the Grail is never mentioned in the prose romances belonging to this cycle, from the *Perlesvaus* onward, which are quite orthodox in their ascetic monasticism.

page 19

a They called themselves *veri* or *boni christiani*, especially after 1165 (cf. A. Borst, op. cit., p. 241), thus emphasizing their claim that theirs was the true faith, in contrast with that of the Catholic clergy (cf. Raffaello Morghen, L'Eresia nel Medio Evo', *Medioevo Cristiano*, Bari, 1951, p. 241 f.). They were commonly called *boni homines* or *bonshommes*, a term borrowed from legal parlance, which therefore implied the idea of justice. It occurs a few times in the form *guoter man* in Wolfram's poem (460, 19; 799, 13; etc.), and is also used to describe the hermit who absolves Parzifal, thus giving rise to a more or less heretical interpretation of this character, see Wapnewski, op. cit., p. 183 f.

page 21

a Baümker, Witelo, p. 357 f. (see note 4*c*). For the prominent rôle played by the Gospel according to St John and the First Epistle of John in Christian and heterodox thought of the twelfth century, and its influence on contemporary poetry, in particular the Grail saga, cf. Wapnewski, op. cit.,

p. 56 f. However, no one has so far applied such considerations to Chrétien's poem, in which traces of the spiritual tendencies of his times are equally evident, although more discreet, and not weighed down by covert allusions and esoteric astrological and religious references of doubtful authenticity, such as abound in Wolfram's poem.

page 22

a For this little-known, yet highly important phenomenon, see P. Alphandéry, 'Le Gnosticisme dans les sectes médiévales latines', *Revue d'Histoire et de Philosophie Religieuses*, VII, 1927, esp. p. 397 f. This article should be supplemented by a study of the influence of Lactantius in medieval Gnostic traditions. This controversial author of the beginning of the fourth century was the first to render the Greek terms γνῶσις or σοφία by the Latin *sapientia*, which he used to signify the divine light that fills man's being and draws him closer to God. On this subject, see Antonie Wlosok's diligent essay, 'Lactanz und die philosophische Gnosis', in *Abhandlungen der Heidelberger Akademie der Wissenschaften*, Phil.-Hist. Classe, 1960, p. 174 f. For the above-mentioned heresiarchs, cf. A. Borst, op. cit., p. 84 f., and the extensive literature on this subject. Similar groups of heretics, who held out for a longer time than their French or Provençal counterparts, also existed in Italy, with such angelical women in their midst: e.g. Fra Dolcino's Margherita, who eloped 'cum aliis IIII domicellis' to follow the friar; then, according to his deposition, 'capta cum aliis et combusta'. Cf. F. Tocco, 'Nuovi documenti sui moti ereticali', in *Archivio Storico Italiano*, 1901, p. 103. For the part played by women in heretical movements of the twelfth and thirteenth centuries, cf. H. Grundmann, *Religiöse Bewegungen im Mittelalter*, (Berlin, 1935, p. 35 f. and passim). This leads one to ask whether the ethereal ladies of the *Dolce Stil Nuovo* and even Dante's Beatrice (a symbol of Sacred Doctrine in

G

the Christian sense) have a precedent in these personifications of divine wisdom, who, superior to the saints and even the angels, act as intermediaries between the supernatural world and blind humanity. For the extent and growth of this phenomenon in Provence in Chrétien's times and its probable echoes in the poetry of the troubadours, cf. Lucie Varga, 'Peire Cardinal était-il hérétique?', *Revue de l'Histoire des Religions*, LIX, 1938, t. 117, pp. 205-31.

page 23

a This setting of Chrétien's story need not appear arbitrary. Such movements were not restricted to the poorer classes of society—as scholars assert who have studied the phenomenon from the sociological point of view (cf. A. Borst, pp. 42-58); they did in fact extend into the bourgeoisie and feudal nobility in Flanders and in southern France, where the castles of the various lords became shelters and strongholds for heretics and anti-Roman faithful (cf. C. Schmidt, op. cit., vol. I, ch. 3, and L. Varga, op. cit., p. 206 f.) just as in the sixteenth century in both France and Italy the courts of Marguerite de Navarre, of Renée de France at Ferrara, and of Giulia Gonzaga at Naples and Fondi were centres for the spiritual life and the intellectual, political, and religious organization of the Protestant Reformation. This phenomenon may be seen even at the very beginning of the heretical movements. The first Italian heretics began their activities in 1028 in the castle at Monforte, near Asti, under the protection of the Countess, widow of Odelrico Manfredi, who followed them to the stake in Piazza Monforte (now Piazza Tricolore), Milan (cf. *Storia di Milano*, vol. III, 1954, p. 63 f. and for later periods H. Grundmann, op. cit., p. 37 f.). The castle of the Grail may therefore be regarded as the poetic expression of a phenomenon that was characteristic of the times, although less obvious than the popular heretical movements, such as the Patarines, the Poor Men of Lyons, the Waldenses, Lombards and other heterodox sects organized from 1170 onward. The part played by the Italian aristocracy in promoting heretical propaganda has been emphasized by G. Volpe, *Movimenti e sette ereticali nella società medievale italiana* (2nd ed. Florence, 1926, p. 185).

page 24

a Various scholars have cast doubt upon this continuity. However, Alphandéry, op. cit., adduces documents to prove how tenacious this covert Gnostic tradition was in medieval France. O. Rahn in his *Kreuzzug gegen den Graal* connects it with the Gallic druids (about whom so little is known), while S. Runciman, *The Medieval Manichee* (Cambridge, 1947), gives a convincing outline of the ideological and doctrinal bonds that link the pseudo-Christian dualism of France and Italy, from the tenth century onward, with Eastern Europe, where it would seem never to have disappeared. We find in this Gnostic-Manichaean tradition a constant attempt to invest it with Christian forms, a tendency found earlier in the Apocryphal Gospels and Acts which, like the writings attributed to Thomas, present the Gnosis in a Christian garb that hardly conceals its pagan character, as has been proved by G. Bornkamm, *Mythos und Legende* ('Forschungen zur Religion und Literatur des Neuen Testaments', vol. 31, Gottingen, 1933). The same phenomenon is found in the Oriental communities of the 'Religion of light' or *Ming Chiao*, so that Marco Polo, on discovering one of these at Fuchow in the province of Fukien, mistook it for a Christian sect, for such it wished to appear in order to escape persecution. Cf. my article on 'Manichaeism, Buddhism and Christianity in Marco Polo's China', *Asiatische Studien (Etudes Asiatiques)*, v, 1951, pp. 1–21. This would explain why the Christian appearances in Chrétien's story on closer inspection turn out to be the symbols and rites of another faith.

b Quoted in the Catharist–Manichaean treatise *Liber de Duobus Principiis*, ed. by A. Dondaine, p. 108 f.

page 25

a Cf. the *Liber de Duobus Principiis*, ed. A. Dondaine, p. 151 f., which, while it is more thoroughly Christianized, nevertheless preserves the ancient Catharist tradition by insisting on the concept of the *panis vitae* and evoking the 'panis de celo descensus' according to St John's Gospel, 6: 26–33 and 42. This concept inspired the famous episode in Wolfram's poem, when a dove brings down a host directly from Heaven and places it upon the Grail, on a Good Friday (Lib. IX, 470, 1 f.), thereby indicating that the consecration of the host does not take place according to the dictates of Catholic liturgy, but directly from Heaven, and illustrating the 'esca angelorum . . . et panis paratus de celo' of the *Liber Sapientiae*, 16, 20–1. H. Folger, O.S.B., in 'Eucharistie und Graal' (*Archiv für Liturgiewissenshaft*, V, 1957, 1, pp. 96–102) offers a clear and concise account of the current interpretations, questions the Grail's supposed relationship with Catholic liturgical tradition and discovers Gnostic influences in a vaguely Christian setting. But neither he nor any of the scholars who have found supposedly heretical elements in the German poem (such as Rahn, Schröder, Zeydlin, and Wapnewski) has ever thought of this 'panis supersubstantialis', as the 'panis vitae' and 'panis de celo' of St John's Gospel, 6: 47–56 (si quis ex ipso manducaverit, non morietur). For the Catharists this signified the 'Lex Christi', but not the 'Corpus Christi' as may be seen from the *Liber de Duobus Principiis*, ed. cit., p. 152 f. This seems to correspond not only to Wolfram's host, but also to that found in Chrétien's *Conte del Graal*. The former receives its consecration from Heaven, the latter from the divine light —which, from both the Catholic and the heterodox point of view, is more or less the same thing. The term 'panis supersubstantialis' is found in St Matthew's Gospel (6: 11). A. Dondaine (ed., *Liber, etc.*, p. 47) asserts in his commentary on the Catharist ritual that with this term 'le réalisme chrétien disparaît totalement'. The term 'quotidianum' occurs in St Luke's Gospel, 11: 3. The discrepancy between the two versions of the Vulgate in the most sacred text of the Gospels is philologically to be explained by the fact that the two terms are more or less conjectural renderings of the rare Greek word 'ἐπιούσιον, whose meaning was uncertain even in early Christian times. Cf. the relevant article in Kittel and Friedrich's *Theologisches Wörterbuch*.

b A. Dondaine, op. cit., p. 65, ll. 25–38. Henry and Renée Kahane in 'Wolframs Gral und Wolframs Kyōt', *Zeitschrift für Deutsches Altertum und Deutsche Literatur*, LXXXIX, 1959, p. 195 f., mention the possibility, at the Byzantine court, of a profane transformation of a sacred receptacle. At the end of an imperial banquet obviously intended to be an agapē, the Basileus consumed a piece of bread presented by a court official in the παναγιάριον, a vessel which roughly corresponds to the 'tailleor' rather than to the Grail, or κρατήρ according to the authors just quoted. But all this is still very doubtful.

page 26

a Cf. the extensive article on Bérenger in the *Dictionnaire de Théologie Catholique* and the essential passages from the texts in C. Mirbt, *Quellen zur Geschichte des Papstums und des Römischen Katholizismus*, 5th ed., Tübingen, 1934, p. 144 f. For Bérenger's influence on the clergy and people of France, associated with that of the Albigensians in the symbol of the 'panis purus' which replaced the 'verum corpus', cf. J. A. Jungmann, S.J., *Missarum Solemnia*, Vienna, 1948, I, p. 151 f., with bibliography, and II, 261 f.

page 30

a These hermits lived on in chivalric poems long after their disappearance from historical reality. The phenomenon died out in France in the twelfth century, whereas in Italy it continued throughout the thirteenth, as certain outstanding cases go to prove. The upsurge of the new religious orders in those centuries absorbed individual cenobitism, whose sociological and psychological background remains obscure, at least as far as France is concerned; it certainly has not been studied as profoundly as its Oriental counterpart (see e.g. the writings of P. Delehaye). As in Chrétien's poem (ll. 623 f.), such hermits, on account of their holy lives and their popularity, enjoyed the favour of both princes and nobles in France, who, preferring them at times to ordinary ecclesiastics, would visit their refuges in the depths of the forests and other deserted places, in order to do penance or ask for counsel. See the article *Anachorètes* in the *Dictionnaire de Théologie Catholique*, vol. 1, part 1, col. 1135 f.

page 32

a Other versions given by A. Hilka in his critical edition (l. 3513) have *parmi les quisses* and *parmi les jambes*, the latter repeated from l. 436, which refers to Perceval's father. The various attempts to identify this javelin with the lance carried in the procession are not convincing, for the lance is never referred to by any other name throughout the course of the poem (ll. 3192, 3197, 3240, 3399, 3549, 4737, 6116, 6373, etc.), while no further mention is made of the javelin; nor is it clear why Chrétien, who was well acquainted with the weapons of his age, substituted the one for the other. The Augustinian symbolism of *infixum telum* (see note 34*c*) is better rendered by the javelin than by the lance. Nevertheless, one must take into account the fact that, according to the courtly, chivalric standards accepted and followed by Chrétien, a javelin is a rustic weapon only fit for the hunt (cf. ll. 79, 95 f., 122, 198 f.), unworthy of a knight, and therefore inappropriate to the setting in which the bleeding lance appears during the ceremony at the castle of the Fisher King, where it replaces the javelin. Such an explanation does, in part at least, resolve the verbal incongruity, while it stresses the conceptual affinity between the two weapons.

page 34

a Most critics are agreed on this point. For Wolfram (Lib. IX, 479, l. 3 f.), the wound inflicted on the genitals (*durch die heidruose sîn*, ibid., l. 12) in a fight with a pagan knight is a punishment for the sinner's concupiscence (*Amor was sîn krîe*, ibid., 478, 30, and therefore: 'durch vröude an minnen stiure/ des twanc in der minnen ger', 479, 6–7). The punishment is thus made to fit the crime in a blunt, yet striking, manner. The correct interpretation of Wolfram's term has recently been confirmed by a study of medieval anatomical terminology: as C. Brunel points out in 'Les Hanches du Roi Pêcheur' (*Romania*, LXXXI, 1960, p. 37 f.), it includes 'le duidime, les coullons, la verge', etc., which explains both the expression used and Chrétien's secret intentions, which were then readily comprehensible. Would anyone still dare to link this fictitious fisher-sinner with Jesus Christ? Even in medieval times one did not have to be an expert in anatomy in order to understand the poet's discreet expression 'parmi les hanches anbedues', so crudely rendered by Wolfram.

This is only one of the things that make David C. Fowler's thesis untenable (*Prowess and Charity*, Seattle, University of Washington Press, 1959, p. 30 and passim). According to Fowler, the Fisher King is Perceval's dead father, the two squires that accompany him are his dead brothers, and the penitent 'esperitaus' is a spiritual double of the Fisher King (ibid., p. 55). What a spate of ghosts in this learned interpretation of a simple concrete occurrence described by the poet!

b Such an obvious conclusion only increases one's bewilderment at the obstinacy which certain scholars display in their interpretation of the Grail and the lance as relics of the Last Supper and the Passion respectively. Cf. the late S. Hofer, op. cit., esp. p. 203 f., J. A. Jungmann, S.J., op. cit., I, 153, n. 96, as well as the writings of Mme Lot-Borodine and others, less prudent than J. Frappier (*Chrétien de Troyes, etc.*, pp. 187–96) who at least makes some reservations regarding the Eucharistic and liturgical value of the two symbols which, as we have seen, is non-existent. The Biblical meditations of Sister N. Amelia Klenke, O.P., and the subtle theological speculations of Mme Lot-Borodine have been assessed once and for all by A. Goosse ('Sur le Graal', in *Lettres Romanes*, XII, 1958, p. 302 f.). In his latest study ('Introduction à l'édition du Roman de Perceval de Chrétien de Troyes', *Romania*, LXXXI, 1960, p. 19 f.) M. Roques assumes an intermediate position: whereas he denies the liturgical value of the procession, he nevertheless considers it 'une représentation figurée de divers articles de la foi', which it certainly is not, if we consider the lack of any ecclesiastical or liturgical symbol or expression, as well as the absence of an act of devotion before the passage of objects which should, by such standards, be sacred and inspire reverence. However, the experts' ambiguous interpretations and hesitation are due to the ambiguity and occasional ambivalence inherent in the religious symbols of an age that was unsure of their various meanings.

c This is the way in which Wolfram von Eschenbach interpreted it. He insists on the idea of sin and punishment regarding the invalid in the sense illustrated by Wapnewski, op. cit., p. 80 f. St Augustine in his treatise *De Trinitate* several times compares sin to an 'infixum telum'—an image that may well have inspired Chrétien to give symbolic value to the javelin or lance in his poem.

page 36

a Dante clearly tells us so, when, following Aristotle and medieval rhetoric, he states 'nomina sunt consequentia rerum' (*Vita Nuova*, ch. XIII).

This is an *annominatio* characteristic of ancient and medieval rhetoric, of which various examples are to be found in Ernst Robert Curtius, *Europäische Literatur und lateinisches Mittelalter*, Bern, 1948 (2nd ed., 1954) ch. XV, 3. However, Curtius does not point out the essential difference that exists between the rare use of this figure of speech in ancient literature and its abuse on the part of medieval writers. The latter, including Dante, frequently saw in such stylistic ornaments a substantial affinity that went beyond any arbitrary association of sound or meaning. It would be interesting to study their various functions in Dante. This distinction between the two types of *annominatio* must also be kept in mind when considering the other Greek and Latin features listed by Curtius, in order to appreciate the originality of medieval art and the independence of vernacular poetry from its Latin predecessor.

b For the history of this ancient Christogram, cf. F. J. Dölger's fundamental work, *ΙΧΘΥΣ: Das Fischsymbol in der frühchristlichen Zeit*, 4 vols, Rome, Spithöver, 1910 et seq., esp. vol. III. Its application to the Fisher King has been fully discussed by Jessie L. Weston in her book, *From Ritual to Romance*, ch. IX, and accepted more or less explicitly by other critics, none of whom seems to have realized that this is tantamount to identifying the invalid king with Jesus Christ—an unthinkable sacrilege in view of the location and meaning of his wound. In Chrétien's poem (l. 3520 f.) we read that the invalid was fishing 'por ce einsi se deduit'—that is, for mere pleasure—and that he caught a 'poissonet/un petit greignor d'un veironet' (l. 3009), namely, a small fish slightly larger than a minnow (*Cyrpinus phoxinus*). How is it possible to associate such insignificant details with the holy Christogram? Likewise, it is of little avail to evoke vague Celtic myths in an attempt to discover some Irish water-God in this personage, or another derived from a god of fertility, Christianized we know not how or when (cf. W. A. Nitze, 'How Did the Fisher King Get His Name?' in *Medieval Studies in Honor of J. D. M. Ford*, Cambridge, Mass., 1948, p. 177 f., the same author's 'The Fisher King and the Grail in Retrospect', in *Romance Philology*, VI, 1952, p. 14 f., and further anthropological and linguistic speculations in his *Perceval and the Holy Grail*, p. 316 f.). Such hypotheses are the work of scholars who do not know what it means to be a poet, let alone a poet of the twelfth century. Chrétien did not give a name to the Fisher King, who is thus presented not as an individual but as pure symbol, in the sense indicated above. Wolfram, as we have seen, calls him Anfortas and makes him the son of Frimutel, king of the Grail, thereby altering Chrétien's theme and intentions.

page 37

a Unlike Wolfram, Chrétien does not specify the nature of the fault which the Fisher King seems to expiate by his wound. That this is, in the words of Mme Lot-Borodine (*Romania*, LXXVII, 1956, p. 260), 'le châtiment de la concupiscence' is obvious. As we have seen, this is confirmed in a somewhat crude manner by Wolfram von Eschenbach. As far as Perceval is concerned, the poet never states that he is guilty of such a fault. Whether, and to what extent, his amorous dallyings with Blancheflor in the castle at Belrepaire (or Biaurepaire), ll. 2047-69, represent a mortal sin is the subject of a discussion between Sister M. Amelia Klenke, O.P., and Helaine Newstead in *Romance Philology*, VI, 1952-3, p. 173 f., and VII, 1953-4, p. 171 f. What is clear is that Chrétien purposely left it to the reader to settle this problem, typical of the amorous casuistry which delighted the ladies and the knights of those times and for many centuries to come. How differently it was judged by the theologians of the age may be seen from the article *Chasteté* in the *Dictionnaire de Théologie Catholique* (vol. II, 2, 1932, col. 2319 f., art. *Chasteté* and vol. VI, I, 1924, col. 600 f.). The question, considered from the point of view of a layman, is one of those discussed some years later by Andreas Capellanus in his *De amore libri tres*, whose connection with courtly poetry is well known. The case recounted by Chrétien (loc. cit.) is also described by Andreas (Lib. I, ch. 6) in the following terms: 'Et purus quidem amor est, qui omnimodo delectationis affectione duorum amantium corda coniungit. . . . Procedit autum usque ad oris osculum lacertique amplexum et verecundum nudare contactum, extremo praetermisso solatio.' For a full treatment of the subject, see Felix Schloesser, *Andreas Capellanus: Seine Minnelehre und das christliche Weltbild*, Bonn, 1960, p. 118 f. But this is as far as we can go. Who, indeed, will believe that Chrétien's essentially lay mind was versed in such theological subtleties as those attributed to him by the critics? The courts and the society for which he composed his poem at the suggestion of Philip of Flanders were neither schools nor monasteries, although they did participate—more or less superficially—in the spiritual currents and moral problems of the age.

b This concept goes back to St Augustine, who frequently examines the problem in his theological and philosophical works, and particularly in his unending controversy with the Manichaeans, Pelagians, and other heretics who rejected Original Sin in the Christian sense. See esp. the first and fourth parts of the treatise 'De libero arbitrio' in *Œuvres de Saint Augustin*, Ire série, VI. *Dialogues Philosophiques*, s.l., 1941, with French translation, notes, indexes, and bibliography, as well as the tract 'De Natura et Gratia' against Pelagius, in the

Œuvres Complètes, Paris, 1878, vol. xxx, p. 193 f., and, in the same series, vol. xxxvi, the 'Tables Générales' (pp. 438–52) with all the passages referring to the problem. The debate flared up once more in the twelfth century and was centred upon motifs and teachings found in the Saint's writings, as may be seen from the detailed historical and theological account in the *Dictionnaire de Théologie Catholique*, vol. xii, part i, 1933 (cf. the articles 'Péché', section 'Nature et Malice', col. 194 f., 'Péchés de la Sensualité', col. 179 f., 'Ignorance et Malice', col. 194 f., as well as the article 'Péché original', cols. 371 f. and 390 f., for St Augustine, and cols. 435–55 for theologians and schoolmen of the twelfth century. For heretical doctrines of that century regarding sin, and the most recent bibliography, cf. A. Borst, op. cit., pp. 174 f. and 180 f. The Manichaean element in these doctrines is quite evident, in spite of its Augustinian basis, even as this influence helped to mould the polemical background to the Catholic reaction of those times, especially in the discussion of the nature of sin and its remission. According to Manichaean and Catharist tradition, sin originates from the spirit of evil and its power of imprisoning in dark matter the particles of the light-giving substance of good: Christ has shown man the way to liberate these, so as to reconstruct in its entirety the kingdom of good, not by his Passion, but by his teachings and angelic example. One did not have to be a theologian or clerk in those times to be acquainted with these doctrines and tendencies.

c This is the general consensus of opinion, convincingly upheld by E. Hoepffner, in *Colloques*, *etc.*, p. 94 f., who establishes the date of the poem at the beginning of the thirteenth century, or twenty years after the *Conte del Graal*. S. Hofer, op. cit., pp. 225–36, is almost alone in attempting to prove—against all the available evidence—that the *Conte del Graal* stems from the *Estoire*, obviously in order to emphasize the Christian origin and orthodox meaning of the Grail and its accompanying symbols. He is followed by E. Köhler, 'Ideal und Wirklichkeit in der höfischen Epik', *Beihefte zur Zeitschrift für Romanische Philologie*, 97, Tübingen, 1956, p. 212 f., who by the same token invalidates his own view of the contrast between ideals and reality that supposedly forms the basis of Chrétien's work. If Robert had preceded Chrétien, the episode of the Grail in the latter's *Conte* would appear even more blasphemous, for it would amount to a desecration of the receptacle which, according to Robert, had received the blood of Christ.

page 38

a ll. 2497–512. The name Hebron is an obvious allusion to the son of Caath, a member of the tribe of Levi who guarded, according to Numbers 3: 5 f., 'vasa tabernaculi, servientes in ministerio'. Similarly, his namesake in the *Estoire* is destined to become the custodian of the Grail, another holy receptacle according to this poem. W. A. Nitze, however (ed. *Perlesvaus*, Introduction, p. xii f.), unsuccessfully attempts to discover in the abbreviated form (He)Bron a reference to the Celtic Bran, who guarded the magic cauldron of the Celts, which was, according to this same critic, transformed into a Eucharistic Grail by Robert de Boron. Such flights of fancy (cf. A. C. L. Brown, *Origin of the Grail Legend*, Cambridge, Mass., 1943), based for the most part on a supposed affinity of names, are judged for what they are worth by E. Hoepffner, op. cit. (*Colloques, etc.*, esp. p. 98 f.).

page 40

a For the catalytic action of heretical doctrines on pre-Scholastic Catholic thought and on the organization of the monastic orders, both ancient and new, cf. *Histoire de l'Eglise, publiée sous la direction de* A. Fliche et V. Martin, vol. IX, p. 330 f., and X, p. 112 f., with extensive bibliography; more briefly, J. Guiraud's *Histoire de l'Inquisition au Moyen Age*, Paris, 1935–8, ch. XIII.

b Various Orientalists have attempted to transform this magic bowl, of which copies were to be found in medieval Buddhistic sanctuaries in India and Persia, into a prototype of the Grail (cf. my 'The Crib of Christ and the Bowl of Buddha', *Journal of the American Oriental Society*, LXX, 1950, p. 164), forgetting that Chrétien's Grail is quite different in shape, material, and function.

page 43

a For the political aspects of the anti-heretical struggle in the twelfth century, see the *Histoire de l'Eglise* (quoted in note 40*a* above), vol. IX, esp. p. 347 f., and X, ch. IV, with relevant bibliography in the notes; also J. Guiraud, op. cit., vol. I, who discusses heresy in the various French provinces and the organization of the political and religious repression, especially in central and southern France. C. Schmidt's *Histoire et Doctrine des Cathares*, vol. I, pp. 66–93, deals with the whole country including Flanders and Champagne.

b Cf. C. Schmidt, op. cit., I, p. 91 f. No complete biography of this great prince has so far appeared. The heretical movements and their dramatic repression in Flanders, which became particularly violent after 1184, are discussed neither in A. Cartellieri's *Philipp August* nor in H. van Huette's *Essai sur la Civilisation Flamande*, Louvain, 1898, nor indeed in any of the histories of medieval Flanders, such as M. Kervyn de Lettenhove's authoritative *Histoire de Flandre*, Bruges, 1874, vol. I, lib. VI, or Henri Pirenne, *Histoire de Belgique*, 5th ed., Brussels, 1929, vol. I. Mme Rita Lejeune, however, refers to the problem in 'La date du *Conte du Graal* de Chrétien de Troyes', *Le Moyen Age*, fasc. 1/2, 1954, p. 27 f.

page 44

a Cf. Mary D. Stanger, 'Literary Patronage at the Medieval Court of Flanders', *French Studies*, XI, 1957, p. 214 f., with a useful bibliography. Chrétien de Troyes, together with various other poets and minstrels, was then staying at the court of this devout, brilliant, and ambitious prince, who was nevertheless at times capable of fanatical cruelty. Count Philip also patronized Guiot de Provins (cf. ch. v, Langlois, *La Vie en France au Moyen Age, de la fin du XIIe au milieu du XIVe siècle*, vol. II, p. 63) who ended his life as a monk at Cluny and was well known for his versatility and for his authorship of a satirical and autobiographical *Bible*, ed. by J. Orr in *Les Oeuvres de Guiot de Provins*, Manchester, 1915. Wolfram von Eschenbach asserts that he had taken from this poet certain episodes in his *Parzifal* that are not to be found in Chrétien's *Conte del Graal*, and that he considered Guiot's work to be superior.

However, no trace of a poem on this subject by Guiot has been found. Various scholars have believed in its existence, without being able to prove it: A. T. Hatto's 'Y-a-t'il un Roman du Graal de Kyot le Provençal?' in the *Colloques, etc.*, is the most recent example. I find his arguments inconclusive. The fact to be remembered is that almost all the names in Wolfram's poem that are neither German nor invented by him are exclusively of French, not of Provençal origin. If one more hypothesis were to be added to so many others, we might suggest that possibly Philip of Flanders charged his two protégés to write a poem about the Grail, inspired by the religious controversies and chivalric spirit of the age in which he played such an important rôle. This would perhaps offer a new clue for the solution of this age-old problem.

b For the episode mentioned, cf. ll. 4164–215. S. Hofer's theory (op. cit., p. 190) that it was inspired by lyrical motifs in courtly Provençal poetry (which is doubtful) is not intended to reduce its originality, which Hofer vindicates against R. S. Loomis, who confidently asserts not only that the episode is 'undoubtedly' of Irish origin, but that it is a 'crude' imitation of a passage contained in the Cymric romance *Peredur*. This romance is certainly later than the Conte del Graal, although according to Celtic scholars, it contains some authentic traditional material of the region. This is pure conjecture, and an unlikely one. The charge that the episode is merely a 'crude imitation' simply shows that there is no accounting for tastes. A careful reading of Chrétien's poem would reveal its delicate charm, witness Reto Bezzola's *Le Sens de l'Aventure et de l'Amour (Chrétien de Troyes)*, Paris, 1947, pp. 19–32, who has approached the text with a true understanding of poetry and of the autonomous nature of poetic genius. More recently the problem has been examined by M. de Riquer ('Perceval y las gotas de sangre en la nieve', *Revista de Filologia Española*, XXXIX, 1955, pp. 186–219) who, with his customary learning, connects the episode with the well-known literary theme of the whiteness of snow and the colour of blood as terms of comparison for a description of feminine beauty. But this hackneyed effect has little to do with the visual image created by Chrétien, with the general tone of his account or with the dreamlike atmosphere with which he has surrounded his hero, who wanders without aim, faith, or shelter amidst the marvels of the world and the happenings of everyday life.

c It is very likely that this inspired Wolfram von Eschenbach's description of the *Templeise* (Lib. IX, 444, 23; 468, 28), as he calls the knights of the Grail in his poem. Although they are neither a heretical order nor a complete lay organization, they have nothing to do with the historical Order of Knight Templars, founded in the previous century in the Holy Land and patronized in France by St Bernard. On Wolfram's use of similar 'ornamental' puns see the edition by Bartsch-Marti, vol. III, p. 346.